CW00418051

John Wesley Harding

Bob Dylan meets Kafka in Nashville

Jochen Markhorst

Copyright © 2021 Jochen Markhorst

Cover design Jaap de Vries

All rights reserved.

ISBN: 9798588008839

For Marga,
a real gal I'm lovin'
And Lord I'll love her till I'm dead

Content

I   Tuesday October 17, 1967   1

1   Drifter's Escape

I   Mr Hyde   5
II   "You're nothing but a pack of cards!"   7
III Out of the drawer   9

2   I Dreamed I Saw St. Augustine

I   Scatter My Ashes Anyplace But Utah   12
II   Josef K.   15
III Chicken skin   18

3   The Ballad of Frankie Lee and Judas Priest

I   "Judas Priest!"   20
II   Parables & Paradoxes   22
III Fermate   26
IV   Time is an illusion   28
V   Grace and a fluttering mandolin   31

II   Monday November 6, 1967   34

4   All Along The Watchtower

I   Go Set A Watchman   39
II   Ronk growls   42
III Into the stratosphere   44

5 John Wesley Harding

I	A stout stick	47
II	A throwaway	49
III	Johnny Cash	51
IV	John Hardy	53
V	Thea	56

6 As I Went Out One Morning

I	Last year's vogue writer	58
II	Good dog	61
III	The fairest damsel	65

7 I Pity The Poor Immigrant

I	The cat who said ouch	67
II	Peter Amberley	70
III	Reeds, bass and percussion	72

8 I Am a Lonesome Hobo

I	"Go on, read, it does not say what it says"	75
II	Luke the Hobo	78
III	The Zimmerman Shadow	80

IIII Wednesday November 29, 1967 83

9 The Wicked Messenger

I	Give it up!	87
II	A rather reverse order	89
III	In Schrafft's	92
IV	Wondering Which Way To Go	95

10 I'll Be Your Baby Tonight

I	Blues In The Night	97
II	Slut wives	101
III	All that jazz	103

11 Down Along The Cove

I	Bob Johnston	106
II	The Jacks and the River Queen	109
III	Duane & Duke	113

12 Dear Landlord

I	Neil Young	115
II	Triptych	118
III	Old Man	120

IV Frank is the key   122

Sources   127

I'm not in the songs anymore

What I do know is that I put myself out of the songs. I'm not in the songs anymore, I'm just there singing them, and I'm not personally connected with them. I write them all now at a different time than when I record them. It used to be, if I would sing, I'd get a verse and go on and wait for it to come out as the music was there, and sure enough, something would come out, but in the end, I would be deluded in those songs. Besides singing them, I'd be in there acting them out – just pulling them off. Now I have enough time to write the song and not think about being in it.

Bob Dylan, *John Cohen and Happy Traum interview*, June/July 1968

I   Tuesday October 17, 1967

The Summer Of Love passes Bob Dylan by, pretty much unnoticed. Elsewhere Sergeant Pepper converts the music scene to sitar, trumpets, sound effects, strings, studio experiments, psychedelics at all. Pied pipers sit on surreal pillows at the gates of dawn, satanic majesties put flowers in their hair and go to San Francisco.

Not Dylan. After a minor, though mythologised motorbike accident in July '66, *the hippest person on earth* (according to Marianne Faithfull) withdraws from the rat-race, the drugs and the exhausting vortex of recordings, concert tours and media appearances, thus probably saving his life. Dylan and The Band spend months in the countryside near Woodstock in a big pink house, playing antique folk songs and country songs in the basement. Accompanied by his four comrades, he also tinkers with some seventy songs of his own that sound fresh and old-fashioned at the same time. Some of them are gratefully picked up by others. Manfred Mann scores with "The Mighty Quinn", Julie Driscoll has a hit with "This Wheel's On Fire", The Byrds are happy with "You Ain't Going Nowhere" and half the music world throws itself "I Shall Be Released", to name but a few. As for the originals: the world has to make do with sneaky bootleg recordings - especially *The Great White Wonder* achieves mythical status.

In October and November '67, Dylan interrupts his fun in and outside the Big Pink with three serious recording sessions in Nashville.

A year and a half ago Dylan recorded *Blonde On Blonde* in Nashville, also with producer Bob Johnston, and back there, they haven't forgotten that yet. Multi-instrumentalist and undisputed leader of the session musicians The Nashville Cats, Charlie McCoy, tells in an interview with *The Independent* (June 2015) about the culture shock Dylan brought about in Nashville:

> We sat there from 2pm till 4am the next morning and we never played a note. This was unheard of, everybody was on the clock. We couldn't believe it. You're figuring out ways to stay awake because he might decide at any minute that he wanted to record and we wanted to be ready for him.
> I don't know how many games of ping pong we must have played. Then at 4am he came up with "Sad-Eyed Lady of the Lowlands", an 11-minute ballad. And everybody's sitting there saying, "Please don't let me make a mistake." He just started playing it and kind of left it up to us to decide what to do. Every recording, there was no conversation.

"That was the introduction to Bob Dylan," McCoy says, "that's something you don't forget." And drummer Kenny Buttrey hasn't forgotten the experience either. So when he gets a call from producer Johnston a year and a half later, he immediately goes into training. According to biographer Blumenstein, he sleeps fifteen hours a day and stockpiles a supply of amphetamine pills through befriended truck drivers, in order to be able to cope with the gruelling nights of recording a Dylan record.

That turns out to be unnecessary. The Dylan reporting for duty in Nashville at the end of October is, in every respect, a different Dylan from the rushed, wrinkled and dishevelled bohemian of eighteen months ago. *This* Dylan is a married housefather with a beard, a different voice and a rather neat haircut, and actually arrives prepared; the lyrics have already been written.

One biographer, the usually thoroughly researching Sid Griffin in his beautiful book *Million Dollar Bash* (second edition, 2014), reports the detail that Dylan travels to Nashville by train - a journey of more than two days in those days. Which is a romantic image: Dylan, alone in a private compartment, writing the texts for *John Wesley Harding* in his notebook, Bible on the folding table.

The accompanying melodies Dylan plucks from the air, on the spot, just like in the *Basement*. "We just flew through that stuff," says McCoy, and to biographer Sounes drummer Kenny Buttrey confirms this in similar terms:

"We went in and knocked 'em out like demos," says Buttrey. "It seemed to be the rougher the better. He would hear a mistake and laugh a little bit to himself as if [to say], *Great, man, that's just great. Just what I'm looking for.*"

That first day of recording is the 17th, the third Tuesday of October 1967. In Beijing that morning Puyi dies, the twelfth emperor of the Qing dynasty, *The Last Emperor* Xuantong, whose life will be filmed in 1987 by Bernardo Bertolucci (*L'Ultimo Imperatore*). Lulu leads the Billboard Hot 100 with "To Sir, With Love". Off-Broadway is the premiere of *Hair*. In London is the memorial service for Beatles manager Brian Epstein.

The weather in Nashville is pleasant; dry, around 65°. At 9 o'clock in the evening the three men start recording for the album that will turn out to be *John Wesley Harding*.

The studio logs confirm the memories of Buttrey and McCoy: the session lasts only three hours (9pm – midnight). Three songs are recorded:

1. Drifter's Escape

2. I Dreamed I Saw St. Augustine

3. The Ballad Of Frankie Lee And Judas Priest

Bob Dylan (guitar, harmonica),
Charlie McCoy (bass),
Kenny Buttrey (drums),
Producer Bob Johnston

1   Drifter's Escape

I   Mr Hyde

When Jack Fate, Dylan's alter ego, starts "Drifter's Escape" with his band, in the dusky film *Masked And Anonymous* (2003), the fair Pagan Lace (Penelope Cruz), seated between the Pope and Gandhi sighs: "I love his songs 'cause they're not precise. They're emotionally ambiguous. They invite different interpretations."

That does not stop Uncle Sweetheart (John Goodman) from explaining, completely clear and free of doubts, what this song is about. But first his interlocutor Bobby Cupid (Luke Wilson) may reveal what he thinks. "It's about trying to get to heaven. You have to know the route before you start out," Bobby firmly states, and gets haughtily dismissed by know-it-all Sweetheart:

No, it' s not about that at all. What strikes you about the song is the Jekyll-and-Hyde-quality. The song is written from Hyde's point of view. That's what you like. It's about doing evil and trying to kill your conscience if you can. It's not like those other songs of his, the ones about faithless women and booze, brothels, and the cruelty of society. It's not like those. This one's right up your alley. It's about doing good by manipulating the forces of evil. It's just like you.

Goodman differs in detail from the script and the superfluous punch line is even completely cut out ("*Robert Louis Stevenson, it's everything he was saying and more*"). Moreover, he contradicts himself (first, it is about "doing evil", four lines later it is suddenly about "doing good"). But the core idea remains intact, whether it is about "doing good by manipulating the forces of evil" or about "doing evil and killing your conscience if you can", according to Sweetheart it is in any case about the battle between Good and Evil. Food for Dylanologists, because Dylan has (partly) written the script, so the exegetes get a rare gift here: the master himself shares a vision on one of his songs. Entirely in style, fortunately - it does not get much clearer.

Sweethearts assertion that the song is written from Hyde's perspective, does not seem to be maintainable. The second line of the song (*I heard the drifter say*) shows the narrative perspective: an otherwise nameless "I" reports. The I-person does not seem to have any guiding role or any influence on the action at all. In fact, no actor in "Drifter's Escape" is eligible for a comparison with the pure, unscrupulous evil done by Mr Hyde in Stevenson's novella (*The*

Strange Case of Dr Jekyll and Mr Hyde, 1886) is personified. If you really want to see a parallel, then at most Dr Jekyll qualifies. The Drifter has no idea what the problem is ("*I still do not know what it was that I've done wrong*"), just like Dr Jekyll was not aware of the evil he had done while being Mr Hyde. The other lines of the wanderer's text suit Dr Jekyll as well. The respected physician accuses himself of weakness ("*in an hour of moral weakness, I once again compounded and swallowed the transforming draft*"), knows that he does not have much time left and looks back with disgust at the trip he has made as Mr Hyde.

Additionally, the aphoristic point made by Sweetheart then is the wrong way around. Dr Jekyll has to manipulate the forces of *good* in order to be able to do evil. Sweetheart confuses both main characters, or he thinks of one of the best-known one-liners from the German satirist Wilhelm Busch: *Das Gute, dieser Satz steht fest, ist stets das Böse was man läßt* ("What is Good, this much is true, is the Evil that we don't do").

II   "You're nothing but a pack of cards!"

It seems therefore, at first, that Dylan, through Uncle Sweetheart, once again raises one of his beloved smokescreens to tease the analysts, giving - successfully - a mere *suggestion* of ethical depth to this half-forgotten miniature from 1967. But if we go along with it anyway, there is only one option left: the "I" from line two is a Mr. Hyde, is the Evil in oneself. The dormant "Mr. Hyde" currently has no control over the body in which he is residing, the body of the Drifter, and notes with distance, in the third person, what is happening to his host. In any case, that is consistent with the narrative style in Stevenson's masterpiece; in it the unfortunate doctor and his evil alter ego also speak about each other in the third person.

Nevertheless, this song is *not* about the biblical question of what Good and Evil is, the lyrics do not trigger any reflection on ethics. A judge, a jury, a not-understanding convict ... the theme of this parable-like story is of course *guilt*, thus leading us to Kafka.

In his *Er. Aufzeichnungen aus dem Jahre 1920* Kafka thinks back to an insight that he already had as a young adult in 1898. At that moment, Kafka already knows that he will become a writer, and even what his literary output will look like. Literature in which life knows its normal trial and error, but at the same time is seen "as a nothing, as a dream, as a hover", as a realistically described irreality, in other words. The adult Kafka succeeds. Not only in many of his short stories, but perhaps even more so in his three novels, of which *Der Prozeß* ("The Trial") is the best known. That novel is responsible for the many Kafka references in the interpretations of "Drifter's Escape". After all, in *Der Prozeß* a protagonist, Josef K., is arrested and convicted without being told what he is accused of or why he is guilty.

However, this is not *the* Kafka connection. It is really in the Kafkaesque tone that Dylan manages to strike, that unreal, dream-like atmosphere, which we recognize not only from Kafka's work, but also from other songs on *John Wesley Harding* and from *Alice In Wonderland*. The approach is: the reader and the main character share the same pattern of expectations, follow the same logic and share similar norms - and that whole package clashes with a different culture, a culture that is shared by all the other characters in the story.

Alice remains, with the reader, amazed at the actions, the answers and the logic of the inhabitants of Wonderland, just as Josef K.'s lack of understanding is completely transparent to our eyes, but in the meantime, he is all alone in a complex of norms, logic and inference that is obvious to everyone but him. The trial against the Drifter and the ending are, for us in any case, as chaotic and confusing as the court scene in Alice In Wonderland, in the final chapter. Shouting, tumult and disrespectful behaviour plus a closing *deus ex machina*; Alice escapes by waking up, in "Drifter's Escape" the lightning strikes.

III   Out of the drawer

The advocates of autobiographical interpretation do not care for Kafka, Stevenson or Alice in Wonderland. To them, it is evident: the Drifter is the exhausted, unhinged Dylan of

1966, the jury represents his demanding environment of fans, managers and record company and the lightning strike is the motorcycle accident that frees him, giving him the chance to escape from that madhouse. Fits pretty well.

On *John Wesley Harding*, the song is, like the rest of the album, a sparsely orchestrated miniature. Its beauty seems to escape Dylan. It takes no less than twenty-five years before he puts it on his setlist, and then only because of a recent event: the whole country is turned upside down because of the lawsuit against the officers who have abused Rodney King. The riots of April 29, 1992 in Los Angeles inspire the master to pull that song with the verses *The trial was bad enough / But this is ten times worse* out of the drawer.

The live versions are successful, and Dylan gets hooked. Until 2005 he plays "Drifter's Escape" 257 times. Wonderful, but on stage, in the electric version, the intimacy of that studio recording from 1967 evaporates.

This also applies to most covers. Only a few artists keep it small and acoustic, but most of the interpreters, just like Dylan himself in *Masked and Anonymous*, turn it into a rocker, with a variety of ferocious guitars and thunder of drums. The funky accent of Jimi Hendrix is quite attractive, the country undercurrent in Patti Smith's cover is beautiful too, but the most breath-taking cover is the driving, pulsating – quite different from Dylan's original, actually – interpretation by, as often, Thea Gilmore. Steaming and exciting, to be found on the exquisite tribute album *John Wesley Harding.*

Returning to the mystical quality and equally gorgeous is the one from veteran boogie-bluesman George Thorogood. The Delawarean cheats a little by secretly adding an extra chord (in the short, instrumental intermezzi between the verses), but that does not spoil the fun; George Thorogood and The Destroyers on *The Hard Stuff*, 2006.

Amusing is the reference in the opening bars. We hear, quite clearly, Thorogood asking producer Jim Gaines: "Is it rolling, Jim?", playfully recalling Dylan's audible question "Is it rolling, Bob?", meaning producer Bob Johnson, on the intro to the song "To Be Alone With You" on *Nashville Skyline,* 1969.

2   I Dreamed I Saw St. Augustine

I   Scatter My Ashes Anyplace But Utah

The American writer Joe Hill has been successful for a while, not only as an author of popular comics (the *Locke & Key* series, for example), but also as a writer of horror, thriller and fantasy since 1997. Winning him prizes, scoring hefty sales figures and some of his work has already been adapted for film too. His pseudonym is unveiled in 2005 and appears to be not *that* made up; Born in 1972 as Joseph Hillstrom King, he chooses a pseudonym because his father is the world-famous bestselling author Stephen King. Understandably, the young King would like to be judged on his own merits. And from that first name "Joseph Hillstrom" it is only a small, historically correct step to "Joe Hill". Father Stephen and Mother Tabitha (also a talented writer) are admirers of the legendary Swedish-American union activist and honour him by naming their first son after him.

Plus, "Joe King" is a rather unfavourable word combination, obviously.

That Swede is born Joel Emmanuel Hägglund (1879-1915) and emigrates from Stockholm to the United States in 1902. He changes his name to Joseph Hillström, earns a living as a worker criss-crossing the country, in the meantime writing and drawing socially-motivated cartoons, political songs and satirical poems. He is a tough, articulate and intelligent socialist. The latter probably plays a part in his highly dubious death sentence and subsequent execution, November 19, 1915, for the murder of a grocer and his son in Salt Lake City, Utah. On the night of the murder, Joseph Hillström, aka Joe Hill, reports to a local doctor with a gunshot wound in his hand that he refuses to explain - which is about the only incriminating fact on which he is convicted.

Years later, it turns out that Hill's hand had been wounded in a fight over a woman, Hilda Erickson, who in a retrieved letter also recounts that Joe was shot by her ex-fiancé.

Hill's handwritten last will is a poem that once again demonstrates his talent for pointed sketches in a firm, witty style. It opens with:

> My will is easy to decide
> For there is nothing to divide
> My kin don't need to fuss and moan
> "Moss does not cling to rolling stone"

The entire poem is set to music decades later by Ethel Raim, who sometimes with her Pennywhistlers shares the stage with Dylan. Immortal, however, is the tragic, gifted Joe

Hill mainly from "I Dreamed I Saw Joe Hill Last Night", the song Earl Robinson made of Alfred Hayes' poem in 1936. Pete Seeger sings it, Bruce Springsteen plays the song live, very Dylanesque with acoustic guitar and harmonica (2014), but the most famous version is by Joan Baez, Woodstock '69.

Dylan himself reflects on the song in his autobiography *Chronicles*. Quite extensively, as a matter of fact. It is a fascinating passage in Chapter 2, "The Lost Land", in which he tries to recall how he started songwriting. The song "I Dreamed I Saw Joe Hill Last Night" and the story behind it is a trigger, at any case. The life story of the activist immigrant fascinates him, but Dylan then retells it with remarkably little accuracy. For example, he casually mentions that Joe Hill fought in the Mexican War - that war was thirty years before the birth of the Swede. And Dylan tells that Hill was hanged and with his head in the noose spoke his last words, "Scatter my ashes anywhere but Utah."

Joe was not hanged, but shot, and his last words were: "Fire - go on and fire!"

A few years later, when radio maker Dylan plays the Baez version of "Joe Hill" in his *Theme Time Radio Hour* (episode 73: "Joe"), he apparently has been updated, he corrects the inaccuracies and tells the historically correct story.

Dylan ponders on that song. It doesn't do Joe Hill justice, he says. He would do it differently and immortalize Hill more like a Jesse James or a Casey Jones. That would also create a nice circle; one of Hillström's better known songs is called "Casey Jones - The Union Cap". Dylan already has a title:

"Scatter My Ashes Anyplace But Utah", and after that he considers modelling that song about Joe Hill on "Long Black Veil". But alas, although he says he is thinking about how to approach such a first self-written song, it never comes that far. *I didn't compose a song for Joe Hill.*

Well, not in those embryonic years anyway, the artist means. In 1967 the old fascination flares up again, when Joe Hill under yet another new alias finds a place on this beautiful album full of itinerant vagabonds, martyrs and outlaws, on *John Wesley Harding.*

II   Josef K.

The genesis is romantic. Dylan interrupts his months of playtime with the guys from The Band in West Saugerties and gets on the train to Nashville. That is a journey of some two days and it is tempting to think that Dylan is sitting there in a coupe, writing in his notebook the lyrics for the upcoming LP. In any case, there is no trace of it on *The Basement Tapes* and Band member Robbie Robertson also knows for sure Dylan did not play anything of *John Wesley Harding* in the basement of the *Big Pink*. On the other hand, we have the testimony of mother Beatty Zimmerman, who in those days regularly stays with Dylan's young family: Bob "continuously getting up and going over to refer to something" in the "huge" King James Version of the Bible that is always open, on a stand in the middle of his study.

Half quotes, Bible references, and Biblical language at all - it is all to be found on *John Wesley Harding*, so that notebook probably says a few things - which then gets completed on the train or at Nashville's Ramada Inn, where Dylan is staying.

Very different from *Blonde On Blonde*, as the studio musicians and producer of that previous masterpiece also notice. During the recordings for that LP, the musicians played cards and ping-pong for days while Dylan wrote the songs in the studio, there was no limit to studio time and plenty of room for experimenting with arrangements and deviating instrumentation. This time around, the songs are already finished and recorded in no time, with a minimum of instrumentation - apart from a single steel guitar in the last two songs, the job is done by just bassist Charlie McCoy, drummer Kenny Buttrey and Dylan. "I Dreamed I Saw St. Augustine" is taped immediately during the first session, October 17, 1967. And in the same session, which lasts only three hours, "Drifter's Escape" and "The Ballad of Frankie Lee and Judas Priest" are recorded too.

Of course, Dylan borrows the title, the opening lines and the circle structure from *Joe Hill*, but otherwise, as promised, he takes a completely different approach. In line with the majority of the songs on *John Wesley Harding*, the language is archaic, taken from the King James Version of the Old Testament. Here Dylan draws primarily from the Book of Daniel, it seems; that book describes many visions and dreams anyway, and in there we also come across the three kings from the LP's liner notes, the exclamations *Lo* and *Behold*, which Dylan saves for the *Basement Tapes* song, but especially that remarkable idiom. *Ye, gifted, arise, utmost, fiery*, just to name a few. Dylan has to bend over backwards every now and then to get those words in and may still slip one or two times ("*whom* already have been sold"?), but apparently the poet thinks evoking the Scriptural sphere is more important than flawless grammar.

Either way, it works. And then partly thanks to the Kafka-affiliated style and theme. In terms of content, the lyrics have the same opaque clarity, the realistically described irreality as *Der Prozeß* (The Trial). Therein, the main character Josef K. is in the same state of upheaval as the I-person here; feeling guilty without being guilty, and also ending up lonely, anxious and in shame.

Dylan's choice of perspective is a great find and comes close to his envisioned ideal from *Chronicles*. The protest song shouldn't be preachy, he argues, not one-dimensional. "You have to show people a side of themselves that they don't know is there."

In *St. Augustine*, the protagonist dreams that he was on the jury that sentenced Joe Hill to death, and now is consumed by the insight that he killed an innocent, a saint even. The ambiguity is masterful; the narrator *dreams* having a vision. The shame, loneliness and anger are real, but the reason is not - after all, it is just a dream. Only apparently unambiguous is the name; however, this St. Augustine has nothing to do with a historical Saint Augustine - the same applies here as with the names in the songs "John Wesley Harding" and "As I Went Out One Morning", as with the landlord in "Dear Landlord" or Kafka's parables and the New Testament parables: Go on, read, it does not say what it says.

The chosen musical accompaniment is sparse and brilliant. In the original, the slow waltz which Dylan will make from it just two years later (with The Band on the Isle of Wight), already shines through - the ripening process has done the song good.

III   Chicken skin

The cover versions are almost always compelling. The men of the English / Australian ensemble The Fatal Shore build a stately cathedral of the song on their debut album (1997), the sympathetic Dirty Projectors record a warm, intimate living room version in 2010 and Thea Gilmore's spine-chilling approach (*Songs From The Gutter*, 2005) gave her the courage to venture into an integral version of *John Wesley Harding* (2011, a glorious and brave album) a few years later. John Doe's cover on the *I'm Not There* soundtrack ('07) may be a bit overcrowded, but remarkable it is still, as it contains both echoes from The Band and *Slow Train Coming*. And even Joan Baez's approach is tolerable for the Dylan fan with Baez allergy, on her Dylan tribute *Any Day Now* - incidentally with the original drummer, Kenny Buttrey, and again recorded at Nashville's Columbia Studios (1968).

The most intriguing cover comes from an old slow hand and is on *I Still Do* (2016). It sounds like Eric Clapton unearthed a lost track from Ry Cooder's chef d'oeuvre *Chicken Skin Music* and then livened it up with his own chicken skin inducing guitar playing. Dramaturgically, Clapton's singing does not come close to Dylan, obviously, but he knows quite well how to uncover the hidden melodic ore deposits - the quality in which Dylan himself has excelled for more than half a century.

3   The Ballad Of Frankie Lee And Judas Priest

I   "Judas Priest!"

In Martin Popoff's *Judas Priest, Heavy Metal Painkillers* (2007), one of the founders of the band, Al Atkins, reveals how they got that band name:

> Bruno, the bass guitarist in Judas Priest #1, came up with the idea when looking for something similar to the Black Sabbath name which we liked at the time. He got it from a Bob Dylan album called *John Wesley Harding*—the song was 'The Ballad of Frankie Lee and Judas Priest'. The curious moniker can be looked upon as a mild exclamation, or the duality of good and bad, Judas being a betrayer of Christ, a priest being a proponent thereof. Just on its own, the religious tone of the name carried a sort of ominous weight.

THE BALLAD OF FRANKIE LEE AND JUDAS PRIEST

... hitting the nail on the head. This plays out in 1969, and in those years, it is trendy to invent a kind of *contradictio in terminis* as a band name, preferably absurd dualities. So, a zeppelin is made of lead, a butterfly is made of iron and an alarm clock is made of strawberry. Metal bands are fond of religious, satanic and dark connotations, resulting in names like Iron Maiden, Black Sabbath and Lucifer's Friend.

Equally, Dylan the Song Poet is attracted to the alienating effect that can be caused by a loaded name. He is chased away from a nice girl by her boyfriend Achilles, a nun is called Jezebel, a neighbour Tom Paine, he marries Isis and a flirty street sweeper is called Cinderella. But even in that - endless - row of alienating names, "Judas Priest" has a special, eccentric power.

Dylan probably already knows the word combination as a civilized expletive, as a "mild exclamation", as Al Atkins calls it; instead of taking His name in vain, like "Jesus Christ!" or "God Almighty!", some decent Christians prefer to use the less blasphemous "Judas Priest!". Main characters in the plays of Sam Shepard, for example (first in *Operation Sidewinder* from 1970, later also in *Buried Child*, '78).

The language artist appreciates, just like hard rock singer Al Atkins does two years later, the inner tension and chooses to elevate the decent curse to the name of a protagonist in his ballad.

"Frankie Lee" is less traceable. Dylan's first association is probably Lightnin' Hopkins cousin, Frankie Lee Sims, of whom he will play "Lucy Mae Blues" and "Walkin' With Frankie" some forty years later in *Theme Time Radio Hour*. And in the second instance perhaps the murderer of "Little Sadie", Lee Brown; *yes sir, my name is Lee* - maybe he is even called Frankie Lee Brown. But both associations the bard probably only has afterwards, reading back - more likely is that the artist chooses an everyday, colourless name as a contrast for that exorbitant "Judas Priest". A Midwestern, farm boy's name, such as "Lucy Mae" or "Bobby Jean" or "Billie Joe". After all, in the ballad Frankie Lee is the somewhat simple loser who goes down, Judas Priest the mysterious, stable counterforce.

II Parables & Paradoxes

"The Ballad Of Frankie Lee And Judas Priest" is the first song Dylan records for *John Wesley Harding* and probably the first song he writes for it. The elaboration and the length differ considerably from the other eleven songs and the song comes close to Dylan's own understanding of a classical ballad:

> When they were singing years ago, it would be as entertainment... a fellow could sit down and sing a song for half an hour, and everybody could listen, and you could form opinions. You'd be waiting to see how it ended, what happened to this person or that person. It would be like going to a movie.
>
> (interview with John Cohen, summer of '68)

Dylan thinks of epic songs, of the long, drawn-out, narrative ballads, rhyming stories to music, such as "Beowulf" and the *Broadsides*. The song "John Wesley Harding" was set up like that too, as he explains in '69 to Rolling Stone's Jann Wenner: "You know, a real long ballad."

In the end most of the "ballads" on *John Wesley Harding* become compressed, parable-like songs of three couplets, more lyrical than epic, which have hardly any common ground with the classical ballads. Only *Frankie Lee and Judas Priest* still does. Somewhat, at least: it is *real long*. Well, quite *long*, anyway.

Yet even with this *real long ballad*, it is not so much the narrative component that dominates, but that parable character. In the same interview with John Cohen, Dylan himself is a bit shy about his knowledge of, or his click with, parables:

> JC: "That's why I gave you Kafka's *Parables and Paradoxes*, because those stories really get to the heart of the matter, and yet you can never really decipher them."
> BD: "Yes, but the only parables that I know are the Biblical parables. I've seen others. Khalil Gibran perhaps... It has a funny aspect to it – you certainly wouldn't find it in the Bible – this type of soul. Now Mr. Kafka comes off a little closer to that."

"A funny aspect". *Funny*? That again indicates a strange sort of congeniality with Kafka. We know from the great Prague writer that he classifies some dialogues, plot twists or situations in his own work as "funny", have been intended as a joke, situations that the average reader would qualify as lurid, uncomfortable or cruel.

In contrast to Kafka and Dylan, the Biblical parables are usually not too enigmatic, at least: not intrinsic. Jesus' parables follow a normal cause-and-effect structure, the action and the plot are clear and logical. A sower sows his seed. Some seed grains end up on rocky soil. Those seeds will not grow and bear no fruit. The other seeds fall on good soil and will bear fruit (Luke 8). No surprises, no absurdities. Problems only arise with the interpretation of the chosen metaphor, are text external.

Dylan's lyrics on *John Wesley Harding* follow Kafka's narrative style: the problems start text-internally. Actions, dialogues and plot turns evade everyday expectations and patterns. A traveller asking the way is laughed at by the police officer (*Gib's auf!*). A gentleman who wants to leave is stopped by his servant, who demands to know where his lordship thinks he is going (*Der Aufbruch*). When Gregor's parents bump into a monstrous giant insect in their son's bedroom, they do *not* think: what is this beast doing here, where is our son? Bizarrely, they think: dear God, our son has turned into a beetle (*Die Verwandlung*).

Because of Kafka's factual, recording style, the reader at first does not notice the illogic in the opponents' actions - thus making the evoked anxiety elusive and all the more nerve-wracking.

In "The Ballad Of Frankie Lee And Judas Priest" Dylan applies the same technique. Just like with Kafka, the logic derails right from the start. Frankie Lee needs money, his friend Judas Priest pulls out a roll of banknotes. But then: Judas puts the money *"on a footstool just above the plotted plains."* A bizarre, unreal location determination. Next, Frankie's actions are disconcerting. Word choice and the continuation of the dialogue suggest that it is important *which* of the ten-dollar banknotes Frankie will choose now. "Make a choice," says Judas. Frankie assumes a thoughtful pose ("put his fingers to his chin") but is unable to choose as long as Judas is watching. Judas is lenient and willing to wait somewhere else, but again underlines that he has some concern regarding which specific banknotes Frankie chooses: "You'd better hurry up and choose which of those bills you want" - as if one ten-dollar bill is "right" and the other "wrong".

This psychedelic *above the plotted plains* is still Dylanesque. It is comparable to illogical location indications such as *inside of Mobile*, or *up on Housing Project Hill*, or *along the watchtower*, or *underneath the apple suckling tree* - locations that can only be found on the map of La La Land, due to semantics or incorrect prepositions.

Kafkaesque, however, is the consequence with which the incongruence (the apparent importance of the "right" banknotes) by both protagonists is maintained as an obviousness, thus clashing with the sense of reality of the reader / listener, thus creating discomfort.

III   Fermate

The following verses deepen this discomfort by assigning "improper" qualifications to the dialogue. Judas says that he will wait for Frankie Lee later on, in "Eternity". "Eternity?" Frankie asks, with "a voice as cold as ice"

A *voice* as cold as ice? Words can be "cold", a look, even a character, but a "cold voice" should be something like an unfriendly, unsympathetic voice - Darth Vader, something like that. And in terms of content equally unfitting. "Surprised" or "amused" or "shocked" - those are qualifications that would match the tone of Frankie's verification question, not "unfriendly".

"Cold" would at least content-wise be appropriate to the following response from Frankie. "Yes, Eternity," says Judas, "though you might call it 'Paradise'."

That does sound a little condescending, and Frankie's reply is accordingly defensive: "I don't call it anything" - this time he does not sound "cold" however, but rather says it "with a smile".

After that, it only gets more tumultuous. Frankie is sitting there on his own, presumably staring at that roll of banknotes, and feels "low and mean" for unclear reasons. A stranger does not just come in, no, he "bursts upon the scene" and approaches Frankie with the wondrous question whether he is "Frankie the gambler, whose father is deceased" - if so: one Priest calls for him, a little down the road. Surprisingly,

Frankie replies that he "recalls this Priest very well" - as if it had been years since he last saw him - to add immediately: "In fact, he just left my sight." Peculiar way to express that someone has just left the room, even more curious after the previous communication that he has not yet forgotten Priest.

On the narrative level, the poet has shifted up a gear again. The derailments are no longer from one sentence to the next, but even within one and the same sentence it starts to grind, logic is lost. Frankie speaks this ambivalent sentence with - incomprehensible - "fear". To which the stranger replies, just as inconceivably, "as quiet as a mouse" ("Yes, that's the one").

We are halfway through, a stylistic rollover is ahead, with this accelerated sequence of incongruities. Time for a breather, for a *fermate*. The poet Dylan feels that too. The seventh verse is on a substantive level driven and hectic, but syntactically "calm"; Frankie's actions follow a recognizable logic and a normal pattern (he panics, drops everything, runs in the right direction and finds Judas). The dialogue then is coherent - Frankie's question is appropriate ("What kind of house is this?"), Judas' answer is surprising, but not unrealistic ("This is not a house, but a home").

After the *fermate* we can return to *Full Kafka Mode*. In couplets 8, 9 and 10 the mismatches tumble over each other again. On Judas' quasi-ambiguous, little spectacular correction that he is not standing in front of a house, but in front of a home, a trembling Frankie "loses all control over everything he has made" while the "mission bells" sound.

The dreamlike, Kafkaesque atmosphere now being evoked is enhanced by the shadowy, unreal shifts in time and place. In couplets 6 and 7 it is suggested that Frankie and Judas see each other again and converse in the strange house, but in couplet 8 they are suddenly back on the street in front of that same house. It seems to be a brothel - the description ("bright as a sun") refers to the most famous brothel in art history, The House Of The Rising Sun and behind the twenty-four windows are twenty-four ladies.

IV   Time is an illusion

Equally unreal is the subsequent time warp. In Frankie Lee's reality, sixteen days and nights seem to pass, in which he runs a clearly exhausting and ultimately fatal, orgasmic marathon through that brothel, but Judas, apparently in a different time zone, is still waiting at the bottom of the stairs, waiting to receive him on Day Seventeen.

Just like in couplet 6, the poet is now gearing up again; from couplet 10 the logic does not crash from one line to the other, but within one and the same line:

No one tried to say a thing
When they took him out in jest

"Nobody said anything" would be a normal stage direction for this sad scene, but Dylan nuances: "No one *tried* to say a thing," while Frankie Lee's corpse is being carried "out in jest". "In jest"? Would it have been more serious, more appropriate, to leave the corpse lying there in the brothel?

No time to reflect thereon; the next enigmatic plot turn again forces away any confusion hereon. Out of nowhere appears "the little neighbor boy" who is also "guilty", but this loaded addition does not get the chance to resonate either, being already drowned out by the intriguing exit of the neighbour boy: "Nothing is revealed," he mumbles, under his breath, on top of that - and in passing, the poet thus smuggles in two of Kafka's main themes (*guilt* and *concealment*).

In accordance though with Biblical parables is the coda - an explicit interpretation, or in this case: a moral. However, that only concerns the form, of course. The content is "normally" Dylanesque, or Kafkaesque, but inscrutable any which way:

> *The moral of this song*
> *Is simply that one should never be*
> *Where one does not belong*
> *So when you see your neighbor carryin' somethin'*
> *Help him with his load*
> *And don't go mistaking Paradise*
> *For that home across the road*

The poet opens his epilogue with a run of the mill greeting card wisdom ('know your place, remember who you are, stay where you belong"). The subsequent wisdom begins with "so", thus promising a conclusion - which does not come. "If your neighbor is carrying something, help him with his load" is not a conclusion from the above, in fact: that "morality" teaches, quite on the contrary, to *not* go to your neighbour, but to stay "where you belong".

The last sentence then opens with "And", suggesting a listing, an addition to the previous appeal to help the neighbour, but alas: again, there is no substantive relationship. "And don't confuse Paradise with that home across the road."

True to form, the moral of "The Ballad Of Frankie Lee And Judas Priest" is a moral lesson not linked to the little that is told.

Inscrutable, all in all, and that has been a deliberate, strategic choice by the Bard. In stylistic terms, he cheats with incorrect, and therefore confusing, prepositions and conjunctions, and illogical adjectives and adverbs.

In terms of content, he also interlaces the "ballad" with suggestive, symbolic power insinuating accents that force interpretation attempts into distant blind alleys. Biblical of course, by naming Judas Priest, by the capitalization of Paradise and Eternity, by insinuating number symbolism (sixteen symbolizing 'Love', seventeen 'Victory' and twenty-four 'Priesthood' - a seasoned Dylanologist should be able to deduce some heads and tails out of it) and through the paraphrases. Remarkable idioms such as *foolish pride*, *foaming at the mouth* and *helping with load* can all be found in the Book of Books.

Smoke curtains and fog clouds. Masked and anonymous. A classical ballad, an epic poem with a beginning and an end and a real narrative like "Lily, Rosemary And The Jack Of Hearts" is merely suggested, but evaporates behind an accumulation of non-sequiturs, misleading stage directions and irrelevant details ... masterfully disguised as a dramatic novella full of Kafkaesque clarity.

V   Grace and a fluttering mandolin

The accompanying music is unambiguously simple. A basic, unadorned chord scheme with just three chords (G-Bm-Am) that is repeated from start to finish without variation (Dylan plays with capo, as with almost every song on *John Wesley Harding*, so in fact it is in C), bass and drums. The only excess is provided by two short, beautiful, harmonica solos.

But in spite of the undeniable beauty and inviting simplicity, length and uniformity seem to deter the colleagues.

There are virtually no covers by artists from the higher divisions. Dozens by YouTube amateurs, usually low-quality labours of love by white, spectacled men in their fifties, and in addition a few perfunctory ones by tribute bands - all negligible too.

Naturally, Thea Gilmore cannot escape the song on her beautiful tribute project, the integral performance of *John Wesley Harding* (2011). Her rendition is graceful. Gilmore artificially adds excitement by raising the tempo and the arrangement, to which she steadily adds instruments, but above all: by cheating with the chord scheme. The seventh verse, the textual pause for breath, is turned into a bridge and that is actually a particularly successful find. It had done Dylan's original well, too.

In 1987 Dylan plays the song with Grateful Dead and Jerry Garcia then takes the song back to the studio of his musical friend David Bromberg in the early nineties. Bromberg releases most of his recordings with Garcia only after Jerry's death. Their "The Ballad Of Frankie Lee And Judas Priest" is therefore not released until 2004, on the tasteful, acoustic collection *Been All Around The World*. The men also opt for minimalist instrumentation, but more ornamented (Bromberg lets his mandolin flutter around the melody and the words). The true stronghold is Garcia's hypnotic talk-singing, that more than Dylan's words seems to tell a mysterious, moving and exciting story.

Still, mere suggestion, of course.

The final cover is not yet available and must be produced by Judas Priest, obviously. The guys are capable; their cover of Joan Baez's melancholic ode to Dylan "Diamonds And Rust" (on *Sin After Sin*, 1977) is amazingly respectful and equally attractive - and after that name choice the second time the British metal band skims Bob Dylan. That cover will come, eventually.

II   Monday November 6, 1967

After those first three songs, Dylan travels back, probably Wednesday 18 October, the thousand miles from Nashville to West Saugerties. He is a housefather, Sara gave birth to their second child on 11 July (daughter Anna Lea, after son Jesse, 6 January '66), so there is plenty to do at home. And in between he also dives into the Basement every once in a while with the boys of The Band (or rather, at that time: *The Hawks*). Not the "real" Basement, by the way. Sometime in October the men leave the Big Pink. The instruments and the tape recorders are transferred to the house of Levon Helm and Rick Danko on Wittenberg Road.

Reliable documentation about the recordings of *The Basement Tapes* does not exist, but thanks to interviews and through the autobiographies of Levon Helm and Robbie Robertson, at least a few benchmarks can be set. Levon has been away for months and will return around Halloween (31 October). The basement songs with which Levon plays along have been recorded after Dylan's first *John Wesley Harding* session. The rockabilly-ish throwaway "Silent Weekend", the beautiful soul song "All You Have To Do Is Dream", and Robertson remembers "Santa Fe" as well:

> After a smoke break, Bob pulled a new lyric sheet out of the typewriter and we kicked into "Santa Fe," the beginning of a pretty good song possibility. Bob did some of his vibing vocables on words, and we played through it with Levon on drums.
>
> (*Testimony,* 2016)

And from the same source can be deduced that Levon Helm was also at two Basement highlights which, consequently, must have been recorded after Dylan's first *John Wesley Harding* session:

> The next day Rick had a melody and an unusual chord progression for "Wheels on Fire." It took Bob a few times through to get the hang of it, especially the diminished chord in the verse, but he sang it natural as can be. We stepped outside and threw the new football Levon had picked up until we needed a cigarette break. Meanwhile, Bob ripped off another gem on the typewriter called "Odds and Ends" and we tore that one up in the basement before Bob had to go home for dinner.

Sid Griffin, whose research seems more reliable than Robertson's memories, contradicts the latter in his beautiful, rich book *Million Dollar Bash* (second edition 2014); according to his research (and his hearing), "All You Have To Do Is Dream" and "Silent Weekend" are the only Dylan originals recorded with Helm.

As far as content or style is concerned, the Basement songs have little or no common ground with the *John Wesley Harding* songs. At most the sound of *John Wesley Hardin*, with those deforested, bare arrangements, is comparable. Still, the very existence of these songs surprises even a person as directly involved as Robertson:

> Bob mentioned to me that he had made arrangements to go to Nashville again and cut some new songs, different kinds of songs, for his next release. Quite extraordinary, I thought, that Bob already had another batch of material in the works.

... by which Robertson refers to the first recording session in Nashville, i.e. the recordings - as we now know - of "Drifter's Escape", "I Dreamed I Saw St. Augustine" and "The Ballad Of Frankie Lee And Judas Priest". It is, indeed, *quite extraordinary*. Especially because of the enormous artistic gap between both song collections, which nevertheless must have been written at the same time. Actually, only "Open The Door. Homer", in terms of lyrics anyway, approach *John Wesley Harding*. And in terms of atmosphere at most the highlight "I Shall Be Released".

"Open The Door. Homer" is a bit of an intermediate, a bastard son of *The Basement Tapes* and *John Wesley Harding*. Just like almost all the *John Wesley Harding* songs, the song has the three-couplet structure, but unlike almost all the songs on that record, it does have a chorus. The same goes for the content; it's a crossbreed of the carefree, nonsensical language pleasure of Basement songs like "Quinn The Eskimo" and "Lo And Behold!" on the one hand, and the symbol-loaded, biblical parable quality of *JWH* on the other;

> *There's a certain way*
> *That a man must swim*
> *If he expects to live off*
> *Of the fat of the land*

For example: *To live off of the fat of the land* comes from the Bible (*and I will give you the good of the land of Egypt, and ye shall eat the fat of the land*, Gen. 45:18), but the connection with the limiting condition, that you must "swim in a certain way," if you want to eat the fat of this land, draws that stately Bible paraphrase back to the nonsense. The third verse, on the other hand, does suggest depth. "Take care of all your memories, for you cannot relive them" has an aphoristic quality which is perfectly at home on *John Wesley Harding*. The subsequent Bible paraphrase,

> *Remember when you're out there*
> *Tryin' to heal the sick*
> *That you must always*
> *First forgive them*

... remains completely devoid of a profane or alienating clause, repeating pure and unstained what Jesus does in Matthew 9: *first*, the sins of the cripple are forgiven (Matthew 9:2), only then he is healed (Matthew 9:6) - just as in almost every song on JWH involving Bible quotations.

The other Basement song, the classic "I Shall Be Released", seems perfectly tailored for a prominent place on *John Wesley Harding*. Between the redemption-seeking wanderers, lost souls and ancient archetypes, with the archaic use of words, the Biblical undercurrent and the predominant John The Revelator sphere, the song would have overshadowed "All Along The Watchtower". But alas, according to Cameron Crowe in the booklet accompanying *Biograph* (1985) the song was "finished too late for inclusion" on *John Wesley Harding*, and not until after that is "I Shall Be Released" completed, in the Big Pink basement on Stoll Road in West Saugerties.

That is verifiable nonsense. The copyright for "I Shall Be Released" was established on 9 October 1967 - eight days before 17 October, the first day of recording in Nashville.

Whatever Dylan may have been doing there on Wittenberg Road, out of sight of the others, he is apparently working on five *quite extraordinary* songs, which he reserves for the next recording session, just under three weeks after the first session:

Monday, November 6, 1967

1. All Along The Watchtower

2. John Wesley Harding

3. As I Went Out One Morning

4. I Pity The Poor Immigrant

5. I Am A Lonesome Hobo

Bob Dylan (guitar, harmonica),
Charlie McCoy (bass),
Kenny Buttrey (drums),
Producer Bob Johnston

4 All Along The Watchtower

I   Go Set A Watchman

The scanty instrumentation and the old-fashioned, simple song structures of *The Basement Tapes* Dylan brings along to Nashville, where in October 1967, after a year and a half absence, he finally returns to a real studio to work on a real album. The big difference with those *Basement Tapes* is in the lyrics. The songs in the basement are mostly made up on the spot, done in real time, are nonsense, funny, ceremonial ("I Shall Be Released"), cheerful and even childish. But for the lyrics of *John Wesley Harding* Dylan takes his time - they have been worked on, they were written well before the recordings - incidentally, an unusual modus operandi for the bard.

Just like on *Blonde On Blonde*, the lyrics are still suggestive and elusive, but also much more precise, more resolute and seemingly more understandable. "What I'm trying to do now is not use too many words," Dylan says, according to Wikipedia, Heylin, Marqusee and many other parrots in an interview in 1968, "There's no line that you can stick your finger through, there's no hole in any of the stanzas. There's no blank filler. Each line has something."

The alleged interview itself is untraceable, but the quote does fit. Dylan now avoids the wordy decorations colouring songs like "Visions Of Johanna" and "Desolation Row" - according to this quote, every metaphor, all images, are functional. But even though the poetry is now precise, concise, clear - ambiguous it remains.

It is Kafka all over again. The Kafka who already in 1898, aged 15, had an idea of the literature he wanted to write:

> To describe reality in a realistic way, but at the same time as a "floating nothing", as a clear, lucid dream, so as a realistically perceived irreality.

... from the so-called *Laurenziberg-Erlebnis*, the "Petřín experience" in his *Aufzeichnungen aus dem Jahre 1920*, "*Recordings from the year 1920*".

And, like Kafka, Dylan does not shun references to and use of the Old Testament language.

Mother Beatty Zimmerman confirms that her Bob scrolls through the Bible a lot at that time. It is always open, on a standard in the living room, and Bob "is continuously getting up and going over to refer to something." However, clear, demonstrable Bible references are not really here. In the book of Isaiah (20 and 21) there are a few images to be found (the *barefoot servant*, a few horsemen, a lion and a *watchtower*), but without further relationship with the lyrics. It is an inspiring chapter, apparently; the "sequel" of Harper Lee's masterpiece *To Kill A Mockingbird*, found in 2015, is called *Go Set A Watchman* - a quote from Isaiah 21.

The connection between the Bible book and Harper Lee's youth work (it is actually Lee's first work, the work from which *Mockingbird* was ultimately distilled) is fairly easy to identify. That cannot be done with "All Along The Watchtower". A click with Kafka, with a story like *Der Aufbruch* ("The Departure"), is easier and clearer:

> *I ordered my horse to be brought from the stables. The servant did not understand me. So I went to the stables myself, saddled my horse, and mounted. In the distance I heard the sound of a trumpet, and I asked the servant what it meant. He knew nothing and had heard nothing. At the gate he stopped me and asked: "Where is the master going?" "I don't know," I said, "just away from here, just away from here. Away from here, nothing else, it's the only way I can reach my destination." "So you know your destination?" he asked. "Yes," I replied, "I've just told you. Away-from-here -- that's my destination."*

The miniature illustrates on a microlevel the magical power of Kafka's longer stories and novels. Clear, simple sentences, transparent, accessible language, masking the content's impenetrability at first. The discomfort gradually creeps in - something is off, here. It is only on re-reading one notices: in terms of content, no sentence connects logically with the previous one. The servant doesn't understand him?

He doesn't understand "Get my horse"? Strange. Just as strange as milord's reaction thereon: he goes to the stable himself.

And like this, it goes on. One absurdity, or rather: illogicality follows the other. The servant stops his master and interrogates him, the master allows himself to be stopped and also answers the questions - and those answers, too, are not in line with his own next answer.

Here, Kafka makes fairly explicit what the premise is of his great works: the omission of context. We will never know how and why Gregor Samsa turns into a beetle (*The Metamorphosis*), just as it is not revealed why Josef K. is arrested or what he is accused of (*The Trial*).

II   Ronk growls

Dylan the Poet proceeds in a similar way, in this creative phase. Clear language, short, uncomplicated sentences, but the lack of context makes the narrative inaccessible, unrealistic; like a dream, like a realistically described irreality.

Apparently, the joker perceives the situation in which he and the thief are as threatening, or at least uncomfortable, but the context remains out of the picture for the reader/listener - we only get confusion increasing, presumably metaphorical hints about the circumstances. His wine is drunk by businessmen, farm workers dig his soil.

Even the comforting words of the thief are undoubtedly relevant in his reality, but extra stressing for the reader: *this is not our fate*. "This"? What is *this*? We won't know. The camera swings, two riders arrive in the distance - or are they the joker and the thief, and does the flashback start here?

Others do find Biblical references (*Revelation* is popular) or can interpret biographically. The *businessmen who drink his wine* then are the record company big shots running off with Dylan's earnings, for example, the plowers who "dig my earth" are the artists who try to imitate Dylan. And the inevitable diary diggers, who manage to wriggle out something with Sara, Joan Baez or fumbling with other women (the *wildcats*). Verse lines are shuffled around at the instigation of Dylan himself, who in the interview with John Cohen (1968) says about this song: "Here we have the cycle of events working in a rather reverse order" - the third verse "in fact" being the first.

And a film fan points to the very coincidental similarities with the opening scene of the monumental *The Good, The Bad and The Ugly* (Sergio Leone, 1966); two horsemen are approaching from afar, and lo, the wind is howling and behold, an animal (wildcat?) is snarling aggressively. (But alas: while the film was made in 1966, it was only released in the United States on December 29, 1967 - more than seven weeks after Dylan recorded his song).

Dave Van Ronk, who knows Dylan well, since his first steps in the New York folk scene, has fewer illusions:

> After a while, Dylan discovered that he could get away with anything - he was Bob Dylan and people would take whatever he wrote on faith. So he could do something like *All Along the Watchtower"* which is simply a mistake from the title on down: a watchtower is not a road or a wall, and you can't go along it.

Which also makes curious about Dave's opinion on Kafka's most famous parable *Vor dem Gesetz* ("Before The Law"), from the novel *The Trial* (1925). A persistent countryman waits for years and years "before the Law", because an adamant gatekeeper "cannot grant admittance at the moment".

Probably wrong from the title on down, in Mr. Van Ronk's eyes; "You can't stand *before the Law*."

III   Into the stratosphere

Dylan's tone and instrumentation are perfect. Three chords (in the uncomplicated scheme Am-G-F), drums, bass and a guitar, and an ominous, lugubrious harmonica part. Just like the lyrics, the music promises a climax, an all-encompassing apotheosis which, like the lyrics, never comes.

Most covers, and there are many, many of them, collapse under the tension and end up in a climax, artificially apply suspense (per subsequent verse step-by-step addition of instruments and melody lines is very popular), turning it into a narrative symphony.

Nothing wrong with that by the way - "All Along The Watchtower" is indestructible, every cover has an appeal. If not on an emotional, dramatic level, then at least on a physical level: it is a beloved feet stamper and head banger.

Multi-purpose too, apparently. The song is used in dozens of films, quoted in literature, newspapers and graphic novels, pops up in video games (in *Ghost Recon*, *Just Cause 3* and in *Mafia III*, for example), Hendrix' version is, along with Creedence's "Fortunate Son" more or less compulsory in Vietnam documentaries, the song and the lyrics play an atmospheric or even dialogue-directing role in television series such as *Lucifer*, *The Young Pope* and especially *Battlestar Galactica* (a brilliant, Indian adaptation) and since half a century it is a classic that has been covered hundreds, no thousands of times; from the Olympus (U2, Clapton, Neil Young) via the Tower of Babel (the song has been translated into every conceivable language) down to the school bands in the bicycle cellar: everyone who can hold a guitar succumbs.

The ultimate cover is, obviously, Jimi Hendrix' masterpiece. Even Dylan himself acknowledges that Hendrix' version is more powerful than the original. He not only expresses this recognition in writing (in the liner notes at *Biograph*) and orally, in the MusiCares speech:

> After he became famous, he took some small songs of mine that nobody paid any attention to and pumped them up into the outer limits of the stratosphere and turned them all into classics. I have to thank Jimi, too

... but he demonstrates his admiration too, to this day - Dylan performs "All Along The Watchtower" usually á la Hendrix. And he often does so: he has closed hundreds and hundreds of concerts with it, it is his most performed live song (more than two thousand times).

Never changing the lyrics, by the way.

5   John Wesley Harding

I   A stout stick

"A negro named Mage" gets his face a little scratched in a wrestling match with the 15-year-old John Wesley Hardin and does not handle it in a very mature way, as we can learn from Hardin's posthumously published autobiography *The Life Of John Wesley Hardin*, "as written by himself" (1896). The next day they meet again by chance and Mage wants revenge. He threatens Hardin with "a stout stick" and says he will kill him and throw him into the creek. The teenager Hardin pulls his

Colt .44, says that Mage has to go his way, but in vain. He then shoots several times, Mage goes down and dies shortly thereafter. "That was the first man I ever killed and it nearly distracted my parents."

The memoir is introduced with the promise that the work will shed new light on the desperado, that it will show that Hardin never killed in wanton or cold blood and that these pages will do some justice to his memory.

This intention fails spectacularly. Hardin studied law in prison and that undoubtedly contributed to his ability to express his thoughts, but even with an academic degree he remains an aggressive, hateful and repulsive psychopath, who fails to arouse any sympathy. After that first murder, for example, more black citizens follow, because "if there was anything that could rouse my passion it was seeing imprudent negroes." When he is finally locked up in Huntsville Prison, Texas, in 1878, completely unfairly of course, he counts killing 40 people. The newspaper story that he would have killed six or seven men, just because they snored, annoys him: "That only happened once."

As may be clear, Dylan's John Wesley Harding has little in common with Hardin (the *g* is a misspelling of the bard). Dylan sings of a kind of Robin Hood, helpful and honest, 'a friend of the poor', invents an authentic looking reference to an incident in "Chaynee County" (that name does not exist) and finally paints an elusive Harding. The historic Hardin was repeatedly arrested and eventually spent 17 years behind the bars.

II   A throwaway song

Dylan's preoccupation with outlaws does intrigue. And especially his tendency to upgrade certified nutcases to well-behaved, humane role models. Jesse James gets a single, friendly name check (in "Outlaw Blues") and in "Absolutely Sweet Marie" he plants the paradox *to live outside the law, you must be honest*. A first standard bearer then of that motto is John Wesley Harding. The half-beatification of Billy The Kid (1973) may be attributed to Peckinpah or the angelic aura of protagonist Kris Kristofferson, and with "Hurricane" (1975) Dylan rather sticks out his neck when he passionately defends a man who was been convicted for murder twice, declaring him a hero. A low point reaches the singer with "Joey" (1975), the epic hymn to the immoral Mafioso killer Joey Gallo.

Does Dylan sense a note of unease after the release of the record? He never plays the song, neither is he very affectionate or proud when asked about it. More to the point, Dylan is derogatory. It is actually a failed start to an old-fashioned, long cowboy ballad, he reveals in 1969 to Rolling Stone's Jann Wenner. After one and a half verses he does not feel like it anymore, but because it was "a nice little melody", a tune he does not want to waste, the poet just writes "a quick third verse". Records it and dum-tee-dum, Bob's your uncle. "But it was a silly little song."

It was also the only song that did not seem to fit on the album, Dylan continues, and that is why he places it first and calls the album after the song. That immediately makes it very important, he smiles, and otherwise people would have said it was a throwaway song. The name "John Wesley Harding"? Ah, it fits the tempo and I had it at hand.

Peculiar. It is not the only time Dylan turns away from a song of his own, but there is no song that gets this systematically destroyed by the troubadour.

At least as amazing is the sheer nonsense. The song that does not fit the album is "I'll Be Your Baby Tonight", a second outsider is "Down Along The Cove". The title song fits seamlessly between those other riders, vagrants and desperadoes. And if it really is only about the rhythm of the syllables, the world's best songwriter can effortlessly fit in ten alternatives. John Quincy Adams, George Edwin Butler, James Abram Garfield, John Griffith ("Jack") London … or invent a name if necessary. Joe Franklin Dalton. In the tempo of the song and in the rhythm of the text, there are, of course, endless possibilities.

No, increased insight seems to be a more likely explanation for Dylan's Judas kiss. In the months after the recording, he is probably been made aware about the true nature of Hardin, and an ode to this extreme racist is more painful than ever in the days after the assassination of Martin Luther King (April '68). Especially for a renowned civil rights sympathizer such as Dylan. And presumably, his intellectual pride prevents him from admitting in the interview that he had no idea – hence the flight to transparent excuses and the exile to oblivion.

Pity, nonetheless. The song indeed does have a nice little melody and the lyrics are attractive; the same Kafkaesque clarity that leaves the mystery intact as, for example, "Drifter's Escape".

III   Johnny Cash

The "having the name at hand" is less mysterious: Johnny Cash. *Johnny Cash Sings The Ballads Of The True West* is released in September 1965 and does impress Dylan. It is a double album, held together by a transcending concept; Cash wants to retell the history of the Old Wild West in songs. And it is a prestige project. In the extensive, self-written liner notes, Cash discusses all songs and also writes a long, rather mystifying introduction. In which he explains how he prepared for this album:

> I followed trails in my Jeep and on foot, and I slept under mesquite bushes and in gullies. I heard the timber wolves, looked for golden nuggets in old creek beds, sat for hours beneath a manzanita bush in an ancient Indian burial ground, breathed the west wind and heard the tales it tells only to those who listen.
> I replaced a wooden grave marker of some man in the Arizona who "never made it." I walked across alkali flats where others had walked before me, but hadn't made it.

... and like this, it goes on. To survive, Johnny hunts rabbits with his bowie knife, squeezes moisture out of cacti, almost dies, is saved by a forest ranger at the last minute, but: it was all necessary to empathize with living "the hard way" in the "True West".

In short: blown-up, hyped-up stories that no one believes. But the album is beautiful, and it must have moved Dylan One of the songs that he puts on a pedestal in his Nobel Prize speech, "Streets Of Laredo", is on it, and especially the eighth song, "Hardin Wouldn't Run", strikes a chord.

Cash's comment on "Hardin Wouldn't Run" is just as peculiar as the introductory stories. The song itself is a kind of ode. John Wesley Hardin is above all a proud, powerful gunslinger who does not shy away from a fight (*Hardin wouldn't run*). When he gets out of jail after fifteen years it is the *first free air they let him breathe since he was a kid* and in the end he is shot cowardly from behind without having done anything wrong.

Cash starts his liner notes on this song with: "I wrote this after reading the autobiography John Wesley Hardin wrote just before he was killed" - and that is just as unbelievable as those ferocious survival trip stories.

Merit the song has nonetheless. Daughter Rosanne often performs it; Steve Earle chooses the song for the tribute album *Kindred Spirits* (2002). *And* it does inspire Dylan.

The bard gets further inspiration from his backpack, from his encyclopaedic knowledge of folk songs. In this case from the songs he will distinguish years later, in *Chronicles* and in his Nobel Prize speech, distinguishing them as the songs that are relevant to him and teach him the folk lingo: "John Hardy" and "Wild Colonial Boy".

IV John Hardy

Both *badman songs*, songs like "Stagger Lee" and "Little Sadie", songs that describe life and times and - usually - the downfall of a desperado.

The American version of the Irish-Australian "Wild Colonial Boy" is called "The Wild Montana Boy" and provides the Robin Hood component of Dylan's "John Wesley Harding":

> At the early age of sixteen Jack left his happy home,
> For the sunny shores of Texas he was inclined to roam;
> He robbed the rich and helped the poor, the farms he did destroy,
> He was a terror to old Texas, this wild Montana boy.

Although this can be traced back to "Jesse James" too, of course ("He stole from the rich / And he gave to the poor"). More parallels there are with "John Hardy", the song Dylan plays in the rehearsal room with Grateful Dead in 1987 (and of which there is a beautiful, bluegrassy recording).

"John Hardy" tells the true story of the miner hanged in 1894. For an excellent article in the autumn issue 1919 of the *Journal of American Folk-Lore*, John Harrington Cox plunged into its history. Cox is actually trying to show that the protagonist of the song about the hero with the sledgehammer, John Henry, and the cowardly killer John Hardy are one and the same person. For this he documents himself exhaustively, among other things with eyewitness accounts of the arrest and execution of John Hardy. It is twenty-five years after the event, so many of those involved are still alive. For example, he receives a letter from a certain Ernst I. Kyle:

> John Hardy (colored) killed another Negro over a crap game at Shawnee Camp. This place is now known as Eckman, W.Va. (the name of the P.O.). The Shawnee Coal Company was and is located there. Hardy was tried and convicted in the July term of the McDowell County Criminal Court, and was hanged near the courthouse on Jan. 19, 1894. While in jail, he composed a song entitled 'John Hardy,' and sung it on the scaffold before the execution. He was baptized the day before the execution. This last information I got from W. T. Tabor, who was deputy clerk of the Criminal Court at the time of the trial, and is now engaged in civil engineering. There is no record of the trial of John Hardy in the courthouse. Mr. Tabor informs me that there is no record of the trial in existence. The only thing I could find at the courthouse was the order for John Hardy's execution.

Remarkable is of course the place indication: *Shawnee Camp*. In some song variations it is changed to *Shallow Town*, in others to *a Chinese camp*, but since the real John Hardy was employed by the *Shawnee Coal Company*, since the murder actually took place in Shawnee Camp (the old name for the current Eckner in McDowell County, West Virginia) and because several sources report that Hardy really wrote the song himself, "Shawnee Camp" is the correct place-name. This seems to explain that enigmatic, non-existent "Chaynee County"; just like the spelling error in the name of his protagonist, Dylan writes *Shawnee* phonetically correct, but orthographically incorrect – apparently, he only heard "John Hardy" (from Pete Seeger, for example), and never saw the lyrics on paper. Or, same difference, that other great *badman ballad,* Woody Guthrie's "Pretty Boy Floyd" (*"It was in the town of Shawnee..."*).

The other similarities with the old *badman song* are clearer. First off the name, obviously; the sound resemblance between *John Hardy* and *John Harding* cannot be missed. And in terms of content, there are lines to be drawn as well. The opening, for example:

> *John Hardy was a brave little man,*
> *He carried two guns ev'ry day.*

In 1987, Dylan sings the The Carter Family's version:

> *John Hardy, he was a desp'rate little man,*
> *He carried two guns ev'ry day.*

...and in 1967, for his own badman song, he turns it into:

> *John Wesley Harding*
> *Was a friend to the poor*
> *He trav'led with a gun in ev'ry hand*

The mysterious lady in the second verse can now also be placed. According to folklore, a lady was indeed involved in the run-up to the murder. Hardy had forfeited all his money, on which "a lady" or "his lady" put 50 cents on the table (according to other sources 25 cents, according to the judicial assistant clerk W.T. Tabor 75 cents), so that Hardy could continue playing. He promptly forfeits this friendly gift too, which apparently is the last straw: after this loss he shoots and kills his opponent, *"a Negro boy about 19 years old"*.

In John Hardy's song the lady gets a mention. In the version recorded by the famous Alan Lomax thus:

> *John Hardy was standin' at the barroom door,*
> *He didn't have a hand in the game,*
> *Up stepped his woman and threw down fifty cents,*
> *Says, "Deal my man in the game, Lord, Lord...."*

In other variants it is a whole dollar or even ten dollars from a "yellow girl" (the variant that takes place in "a Chinese camp"), "a silver dollar" deposited by one *Rozella*, and five dollars from "his woman". Dylan undresses her supporting role even further, but still suggests she has something to do with that fatal shooting:

> *With his lady by his side*
> *He took a stand*

V   Thea

Dylan's "John Wesley Harding" has remarkably few followers - apparently the fellow artists have the same moral reserves Dylan has after the recording. However, the only really serious cover is very successful: Thea Gilmore's brave, dazzling project, the complete reinterpretation of the entire album in 2011.

Her delicate, subtle, very well-thought out version of the opening track promotes "John Wesley Harding" to a *real* opening track. The first bars are bare, a sober mandolin instead of Dylan's guitar, in the second verse the organ and mouth organ fall in, some dry percussion and a guitar a little later, plus Thea's shrouded vocals: boy, what a beautiful song it turns out to be.

Still a bunch of lies about a disgusting psychopath, of course, but what the heck.

6   As I Went Out One Morning

I   Last year's vogue writer

Wystan Hugh Auden (1907-1973) does leave a mark on *John Wesley Harding* indeed. For "The Wicked Messenger" Dylan borrows the striking rhyme scheme and structure of Auden's "In Schrafft's", and for "As I Went Out One Morning" the bard even copies rhyme scheme, structure and words from "As I Walked Out One Evening".

Giving some substance to the scornful words that an anonymous critic devotes to Dylan in the article "Public Writer No.1?" in the *New York Times* of December 12, 1965:

Granted, he has an interesting imagination, but his ideas and his techniques are dated and banal--we've been through all this before in the thirties. Like most pop culture heroes, Dylan will soon be forgotten--he'll quickly become last year's vogue writer.

In the same article, W.H. Auden is asked about his opinion on Dylan, whether he sees in Dylan the new *Public Writer No.1.* But the old poet, regrettably, has to pass:

I am afraid I don't know his work at all. But that doesn't mean much--one has so frightfully much to read anyway.

It is not unfriendly; in 1965 the brilliant Anglo-American poet is by no means the only intellectual who really is totally unaware of Dylan or pop culture at all - and he himself stands in the eyes of authoritative literature critics, juries and art tsars miles above the young bard from Duluth. Not that he feels exalted. In her enchanting autobiography, Marianne Faithfull describes cheerfully and with sympathy a meeting with the villainous, provocative Auden:

I remember going to a dinner with Tom Driberg and W.H. Auden. In the middle of the evening Auden turned to me and in a gesture I assume was intended to shock me said, "Tell me, when you travel with drugs, Marianne, do you pack them up your arse?"
"Oh, no, Wystan," I said. "I stash them in my pussy."

At that time (1968) Faithfull idolizes Dylan and she drives her life partner Mick Jagger to the limit by endlessly playing her tape with the fourteen Basement songs. So Dylan may have been discussed during that dinner with Auden too, but unfortunately her book does not tell (*Faithfull. An Autobiography*, 1994, in which she also exuberantly shares her experiences with and observations of Dylan).

Auden's jabbing reminds of how Dylan and his partner in crime Neuwirth try to provoke table mates and other bystanders in the mid-sixties. But both poets are especially comparable at a level above. In terms of status, Auden is still a few steps higher in the pantheon in 1965, but then Dylan catches up with the Englishman. From the twenty-first century the roles have been definitively reversed and now Auden is invariably compared with Dylan. Not only on a literary level, but in particular the man's cultural impact matches:

> In 1939, Auden held a position that can only just be suggested by that of Bob Dylan in 1967: indisputably the voice of his generation, he also wrote in a style so cryptic and allusive that the generation puzzled over what exactly it was that they were supposed to be saying. Something about war and doubt and sex and mining machinery.
> ("The Double Man", *The New Yorker,* 15 September 2002)

Like in *New York Review Of Books* ("an intellectual British 1930s version of Dylan in the early 1960s", October 2015) and in the *LA Weekly* of May 19, 1999, in which additionally a very quotable qualification is added to the comparison:

> "He was not just "the voice of a generation," he was someone whose words lodged themselves in the heads of his contemporaries like shrapnel and remained there for decades afterward."

Auden's "As I Walked Out One Evening" from 1938 consists of four-line couplets in the rhyme scheme *abcb*, exactly the same as Dylan's "As I Went Out One Morning". That is still a fairly classical ballad structure, but remarkably enough Dylan also copies the rather unusual metric pattern: in both works the lines of verse end alternately with an iamb and a trochee.

II   Good dog

In terms of content, there is only a superficial similarity. An I-narrator tells about a chance encounter with a stranger, and in both poems, there is an amorous tension - here the similarity ends. Auden's poem is in fact an allegorical narrative, in which the narrator accidentally overhears a conversation, a conversation between *Love* and *Time* about the power of love, about the issue of whether Love can resist eternity.

Dylan's two major themes, *Love Fades* and *Time Passes*, as is semi-scientifically established by Watson, the talking computer from IBM in the amusing commercial in October 2015.

But not in his own "As I Went Out One Morning". Neither one of the two Great Themes can be distilled from these lyrics, nor any other basic idea. The rather plotless text suggests that Dylan the Poet departed from the same starting point as "Dear Landlord":

> *Dear Landlord* was really just the first line. I woke up one morning with the words on my mind. Then I just figured, what else can I put to it?
>
> (from the *Biograph* booklet, 1985)

... and this time Dylan wakes up with an echo from W.H. Auden's poem on his mind. For the continuation, for the *what-else-can-put-to-it* part, an everyday, domestic scene seems to urge itself upon the poet: he has brought his daughter to the bus stop and on the way back stops by for a cup of coffee at a friendly neighbour. And is then attacked by the dog, something like that.

The narrator walks into the neighbour's yard, where the dog is chained - *the fairest damsel in chains*. Animal lover as he is, he extends his hand to pet, but the bitch immediately snatches and has grabbed the arm of the careless walker - *I offered her my hand, she took me by the arm, she meant to do me harm*. "Let go, stupid animal, *depart from me this moment*, bad dog!" he shouts, startled, but that is not going to happen - *I don't wish to*. The dog is holding on and growling. Almost begging, the narrator now thinks he hears, it seems as if the dog is unhappy and asks if she can go with him. Fortunately, here comes the owner, running from across the field. He furiously commands his dog to let go of the nice neighbour, *commanding her to yield* and finally offers his apologies, as it should be. *I'm sorry for what she's done*, as every dog owner apologizes for the misconduct of his pet.

Dylan the Poet doesn't even have to think about how to upgrade such a trivial story. He chooses archaisms like "*I spied the fairest damsel*" (probably inspired by Jack Elliot's rendition of "East Virginia Blues" – "*There I spied a fair young maiden*") and "*depart from me*" and "*I beg you, sir*", he chooses an antique, Biblical sentence structure and he chooses a historical, highly loaded name like *Tom Paine* for the neighbour.

The setup succeeds brilliantly. The ordinary *dog-bites-man* triviality suddenly is a mysterious, allegorical parable filled with wonderful, poetic power. The Dylanologists are delighted and lose themselves in far-fetched, wide-ranging argumentations to explain what the text "actually" is about. The appearance of "Tom Paine" in particular opens a door that is gratefully trampled down - invariably with references to the scandalous acceptance speech that Dylan gave in '63 when accepting the *Tom Paine Award* from the *National Emergency Civil Liberties Committee*.

Gary Browning sees criticism of "America's constitutive myths" and a reckoning with the "legacy of Tom Paine", without any further explanation (in *The Political Art of Bob Dylan*, 2004). Bert Cartwright sees "Dylan's struggle with the Devil" (*The Telegraph* # 49, summer '94). And at the basis of all the fiercely digging cryptanalysts is of course the confused Alan Weberman, who in the July / August issue '68 of *Broadside* gets all the space to wriggle, bend and turn over backwards in all the twists he needs to prove that the song is a report of Dylan's experiences at the 1963 award ceremony:

> Dylan offered them his world view -- *I offered her my hand*. And the leftists wanted to have Dylan as their exclusive possession -- *She took me by the arm*.

And the "chronology" - the song being on the album's first side - is an "clue to the meaning" as well. In short, it remains puzzling why this Weberman was ever taken seriously by the media.

Incidentally, the dreamlike quality of the song is just as often used to justify failing interpretation - since Lewis Carroll an unsatisfactory, cowardly way out (*"Oh, I've had such a curious dream!" said Alice*).

Then Greil Marcus' commentary on the song is the most sensible. After an example of a possible but vague interpretation (something related to the unraveling of the American myth) Marcus states that the song offers "possibilities rather than facts, like a statue that is not an expenditure of city funds, but a gateway to a vision."

The metaphor is a bit crippled, but the underlying thought is worthwhile: Dylan's texts on *John Wesley Harding* are not encrypted philosophical tracts, encoded political pamphlets or veiled autobiographical confessions. They are neutral colouring pictures; the lines are drawn and everyone may colour it in as it pleases him. *The* right colour does not exist. Not "in fact" either.

III   The fairest damsel

To a certain extent this also applies to the music. Dylan's original is breath-taking in its simplicity and naked beauty. Simple melody, stripped-down chord progression and starkly arranged, like all songs on the album.

Hence, a lot of room for the covers.

The South African Tribe After Tribe produces a tight pop song with reggae undertones (on *Power*, 1985), some restrict themselves to a lonely, solemn piano ballad (Yoni Wolf, 2014), there are derailing, trashy versions, hopping ukulele tunes and dark, gothic readings.

The best covers, however, keep it close to home and choose a country or folk approach.

Mira Billotte's contribution to the *I'm Not There* soundtrack, where it is noticeable that drums and bass copy the original almost one-on-one, is quite nice. Just like Dylan, the acoustic Woven Hand limits itself to guitar, bass and percussion, thus proving once again: less is often more.

Yet the unbeatable Thea Gilmore wins again, with a relatively rigged, sometimes power-rocking version on her admirable tribute project *John Wesley Harding* (2011). The only one who dares to use a harmonica, that's probably it. *And* Thea being the fairest damsel, obviously.

7   I Pity The Poor Immigrant

I   The cat who said ouch

 She is 67 by then, has not been on stage for decades and even longer not in a studio, when hipster Jarvis Cocker (from Pulp) pushes her back into the spotlights. In 2007, for his *Lost Ladies Of Folk* night at the Queen Elizabeth Hall.

Bonnie Dobson performs, of course, her pièce de résistance, the indestructible beauty "Morning Dew" from 1961, unbelievably the first song the then barely 21-year-old Canadian has written. Its exceptional power is recognized almost immediately, and Bonnie's ship comes in; she is included in the folk scene, plays zig-zag through America in the coffee houses, making a $ 125 per week - not bad for such a young girl.

In June '62 she is, according to *Time Magazine*, one of the top female folk artists (together with Baez and Judy Collins), in the - by today's standards - rather sexist article 'The Folk-Girls', in which *Time Magazine* is complimentary, but also analyses:

> It is not absolutely essential to have hair hanging to the waist—but it helps. Other aids: no lipstick, flat shoes, a guitar.

... a guitar apparently being just a little less important than makeup and footwear.

By that time, early 1962, Dobson is already settled in Greenwich Village, where she witnesses the first steps of Simon and Garfunkel (then "Tom & Jerry"), where she shares the stage with Big Joe Williams and Dave Van Ronk , and where she sees Judy Collins and Fred Neil performing her "Morning Dew". And where she meets Bob Dylan.

"I knew Dylan when he was really funny," she teases in almost every interview, *he was absolutely dazzling*, she sometimes adds, still swooning. In one interview (*Etcetera*, April 2016) she tells a little more. She recalls how she and Dylan were once invited for dinner at Gil Turner's:

> Dylan was always at the typewriter and I think that night he was writing *Boots of Spanish Leather* because Suze [*Rotolo, famously pictured on Freewheelin'*] had gone off to Italy and I'd just broken up with the guy I was seeing, so I was also pretty miserable. Not a lot was said that night!

Between the lines Dobson does insinuate having had some sort of relationship with Dylan, but she does not reveal more than this.

Dylan, in any case, is impressed by Bonnie on the artistic level, that much is certain. He attends her performance in Gerde's Folk City, her live album *At Folk City* is on the turntable and he recognizes her talent in interviews: "I took this from Bonnie Dobson's tune, "Peter Amberley", I think the name of it is."

That album leaves more traces, by the way. "Once My True Love" echoes in "Girl From The North Country", "Love Henry" Dylan will record three decades later for *World Gone Wrong*.

With his acknowledged indebtedness to *"Dobson's tune"*, the nineteenth-century folk ballad "Peter Amberley", young Dylan refers to "The Ballad Of Donald White", for which he uses the melody of "Peter Amberley", and will re-use again a few years later, now for "I Pity The Poor Immigrant".

The song, which he apparently got to know in the version of Dobson, is in itself another good example of the re-use of existing melodies, as Bonnie tells in the introductory talk on *At Folk City* (1962):

> "This is a most beautiful song, from Canada, from the East Coast. This is sung by a young man named Peter Amberly, who went to work up in the lumbering woods, in New Brunswick. And the melody might be familiar to many of you: it's the Scottish melody *Come All Ye Tramps and Hawkers*."

In addition to the melody, the lyrics also seem to have inspired Dylan. Though he himself claims to have no clue, as he says when John Cohen asks (*Sing Out*, October '68):

> JC: Could you talk about some of the diverse elements which go into making up one of your songs, using a song from which you have some distance?
>
> BD: Well, there's not much we could talk about – that's the strange aspect about the whole thing. There's nothing you can see. I wouldn't know where to begin.
>
> JC: Take a song like *I Pity The Poor Immigrant*. There might have been a germ that started it.
>
> BD: Yes, the first line.
>
> JC: What experience might have triggered that? Like you kicked the cat who ran away, who said "Ouch!" which reminded you of an immigrant.
>
> BD: To tell you the truth, I have no idea how it comes into my mind.

Cohen's bizarre cross ("a fleeing, *ouch*-saying cat"?) is rather unfathomable and, moreover, disturbing; what else could one answer to that than: *huh*?

Dylan's answer just before that is familiar - he repeats it in the booklet with *Biograph* (1985), as he says a few words regarding the creation of "Dear Landlord": "*Dear Landlord* was really just the first line. I woke up one morning with the words on my mind. Then I just figured, wat else can I put to it?

II   Peter Amberley

So, the first line opens the floodgates. Still, there is a slightly more detailed try to take at the lyrics of the *Poor Immigrant*. Specific wording, the religious connotations and the rhythm of the text are reminiscent of

> *Let me tell you there ain't no room for the hopeless sinner*
> *Who'd hurt all mankind just to save his own*
> *Have some pity on those whose chances grow thinner*
> *'Cause there's no hidin' place against the kingdom's throne*

... of Curtis Mayfield's "People Get Ready" - the song that runs as a silver thread through Dylan's entire career. He already sings it in the Basement in the summer of 1967, again during the Rolling Thunder Revue in '75, in 1989 he records a beautiful studio version for the soundtrack of the film *Flashback*, in '91 the song unexpectedly appears once again on the set list (in Argentina, 8 August, immediately after the equally surprising opening "New Morning") and in the episode "More Trains" of his *Theme Time Radio Hour*, March 2007, radio maker Dylan finds the metaphorical use of "train journey" reason enough to qualify the song as a *train song*, allowing him to play it again. In every single decade of Dylan's long career, "People Get Ready" comes along.

Thematically, however, "Peter Amberley" seems to be the trigger that interviewer John Cohen is looking for. After all, that song is the account of the tragic fate of a pitiful young guy (he is sixteen or seventeen) who leaves home to build a life in New Brunswick and after a few months dies over there in an undefined lumberjack accident. A miserable death, too; Peter's death struggle lasts for days, there are no painkillers, he gets into a delirium and the associated hallucinations and the rave about home and family are eventually processed by his friend John Calhoun in the tragic ballad. All in all, it seems to inspire at least the opening lines of Dylan's ballad:

> I pity the poor immigrant
> Who wishes he would've stayed home

And from there the poet Dylan, presumably, associates on from a rather clean slate. It looks like he has a poetic tone and structure, but he does not compile a literary composition - *we'll see what happens*, we can almost hear the poet thinking.

Twenty-four verse lines, four of which repeat the title. The remaining twenty express the uneasiness of the immigrant in varying degrees of misery, with no further coherence than just that. A tension build-up or even a linear relationship the different forms of malheur do not have.

In terms of content, the poet mainly draws from the Bible. Nine of the nineteen fatalities described are more and less directly traceable. In Leviticus 26 alone three of them (*strength spent in vain, eat but not satisfied* and *sky above like iron*) and all of the others in the Old Testament too (*fill his mouth with laughing* in Job 8, for example, and *build his town with blood* in Micah 3).

Remarkable - again - is a parallel with Kafka. The Immigrant shares two of the ordeals with Kafka's Gregor Samsa, the beetle from *Die Verwandlung* (*The Metamorphosis,* 1915). The lonely suffering Gregor also finds no satisfaction in food ("*das Essen machte ihm bald nicht mehr das geringste Vergnügen* - he was fast losing any interest he had ever taken in food") and likewise loses his eyesight, but still can hear ("*who hears but does not see*"). Dylan's final line fits with some good will to Gregor's end, who peacefully dies contemplating his cruel family "with tenderness and love" ("*his gladness comes to pass*").

Coincidence, probably. Dylan's knowledge of Kafka's work is too superficial to consciously incorporate these kinds of subtleties, but it does once again indicate a kind of artistic connection between the two Jewish greats.

III   Reeds, bass and percussion

The melody, the simple accompaniment and the power of the opening line are irresistible. The colleagues pick up the song immediately after the release of *John Wesley Harding* and cover the song to this day.

Judy Collins and Joan Baez have already recorded it within a year (on *Who Knows Where The Time Goes* and on *Any Day Now* respectively). Thea Gilmore's performance is, as usual, beautiful (both live and on her tribute album *John Wesley Harding*, 2011). Taj Mahal injects soul (recording 1969, released in 2012 on *The Hidden Treasures Of Taj Mahal*) and Richie Havens produces a strangely unstable, yet catchy version, also in 1969 (on *Richard P. Havens, 1983*, the double album with on each side a Beatles cover). Richie Havens' voice usually saves every cover he picks up, but this time he is defeated on that front by Gene Clark.

The ex-Byrd plays a beautiful, perhaps not too imaginative up-tempo *Poor Immigrant* that is only released on the compilation album *Flying High* (1998), demonstrating the same quality as on his cover of "Tears Of Rage": how that heart-breaking, transparent, plaintive voice rises a Dylan song to thin, rarefied heights.

The two most beautiful covers are incomparable. The gospel great Marion Williams sings many Dylan covers, but her "I Pity The Poor Immigrant" stands out above all those covers - a soulful gospel adaptation with a slow dramatic build-up in a Muscle Shoals-y setting; about what Otis or Elvis would make of it, with Jerry Wexler at the helm. The closing song of her great album *The New Message* (1969), the album that opens with her equally superior version of "I Shall Be Released".

The other highlight is instrumental and illustrates Dylan's statement from *Chronicles*: "Musicians have always known that my songs were about more than just words."

With his trio Jewels And Binoculars, jazz grandmaster Michael Moore lovingly raids Dylan's catalogue - *"Explorations of the music of Bob Dylan for reeds, bass and percussion,"* as he calls it. He delivers a masterpiece, the high point of both the album *Jewels And Binoculars* (2003, also including a breathtaking "Dark Eyes" by the way) and the high point of the *Poor Immigrant* covers at all. Bassist and percussionist build a bloodcurdling, disturbing foundation, Moore's lyrical, melancholic and narrative clarinet steps in, and lo and behold, all of a sudden he is here again: the feverish, hallucinating Peter Amberley on his deathbed, deliriously raving,

Who passionately hates his life
And likewise, fears his death.

8   I Am A Lonesome Hobo

I   "Go on, read, it does not say what it says"

 "Many complain that the words of the wise are always merely parables and of no use in daily life, which is the only life we have." Thus, Kafka's parable-like short story *Von den Gleichnissen* ("On Parables", 1922) opens.

In the continuation, the omniscient narrator gives an example of the imagery used by them impractical sages. "Go over" never means that we should cross to an actual place, but rather that we should go to "some fabulous yonder, something unknown to us, something that he cannot designate more precisely either." And the story ends with a short dialogue that is carried out *ad absurdum*:

Concerning this a man once said: Why such reluctance? If
you only followed the parables you yourselves would
become parables and with that rid of all your daily cares.
Another said: I bet that is also a parable.
The first said: You have won.
The second said: But unfortunately only in parable.
The first said: No, in reality: in parable you have lost.

It is the only story in which Kafka thematizes parables
themselves. Kafkaesque is the execution; the great Prague
author casts it in a paradox. The transcending theme we have
come to know from more stories: life as hopeless deadlock is
also a theme of short stories like *A Little Fable* and *Before The
Law*, longer stories like *In The Penal Colony* and novels like *The
Trial*. Atypical, though, is the key sentence of *Von den
Gleichnissen*, which is surprisingly unambiguous and nihilistic:
"All these parables really set out to say merely that the
incomprehensible is incomprehensible, and we know that
already."

In "I Am A Lonesome Hobo" the poet Dylan proves
himself, just like in most songs on *John Wesley Harding*, an art
brother of Kafka, of his parable-like character and ambiguity,
but the paradox is unique - though one could doubt whether it
was deliberately inserted by the poet Dylan.

The poor wanderer tells in the first two verses how he
has lost everything by not adhering to social codes. He had
wealth, family and friends, but was guilty of "bribery, blackmail
and deceit" and now he is lonely and broke. The obvious
conclusion then would have to be: I was stupid, I should have

followed the law, I should have obeyed the codes we all agreed on. But no, paradoxically, amidst all the misery he now experiences, the advice of the repentant sinner is to *not* comply with the codes: "live by no man's code."

The following advice is similarly paradoxical: hold your judgment for yourself - that wisdom the hobo preaches after he has publicly shared his opinion about bribery, extortion and cheating, after he has condemned jealousies as *petty* and has rated his own decline as "shameful". For a man who thinks you should above all keep your judgment to yourself, he is quite outspoken and judgmental.

Inconsequent, or paradoxical, or ... perhaps a thoughtful, extra layer after all? Dylan writes a parable, or at least a parable-like text, and therein the famous definition of Dutch poet Martinus Nijhoff applies: "Go on, read, it does not say what it says." As the etymology also reveals (derived from the Greek *para-bállein* = throwing alongside).

In that case, the hobo does not say what he says, and the readers lands in the same vortex as with Kafka - the clear, powerful sentences suggest a clear, simple message, but confuse by contradicting themselves. Much like in Kafka's shortest prose piece *Die Bäume* ("The Trees"):

> For we are like tree trunks in the snow. In appearance they lie sleekly and a little push should be enough to set them rolling. No, it can't be done, for they are firmly wedded to the ground. But see, even that is only appearance.

A self-contradicting sequence of observations in parable form, just like "I Am A Lonesome Hobo". But unlike Dylan's lyrics, Kafka's text is a fully composed whole; Dylan's paradox is rougher, too sketchy to assume intent.

Probably the creation of this song has been similar to "Dear Landlord" and "I Pity The Poor Immigrant" - the poet Dylan finds a nice, loaded opening sentence and then leaves the tap open.

II   Luke the Hobo

The exceptional talent of a poetic genius like Dylan guarantees fascinating song lyrics, even though the content does perhaps not stand up to the critical review of an academic interpreter.

Hobo as a metaphor is indeed not too original, but in this context, in an archaic-sounding song with austere, acoustic accompaniment, irresistible. And the elevation to metaphor is a trend break in itself, of course, after the dozens of drifters, tramps, ramblers, wanderers and rolling stones that populate Dylan's oeuvre from the six years before - they are all literal vagrants.

In an interview with Melody Maker, May 29, 1965, Ramblin' Jack Elliott remembers how Dylan's repertoire initially seems to consist mainly of *hobo songs*:

> I kind of thought he was imitating Woody but he said he wasn't, that he learned those songs from various hobos he met on the road. So I didn't argue about it. I dug him, and I guess he reminded me of myself a little when I was younger.
> In those days he had a repertoire of wonderful hobo songs, some of which I had never heard before.

The hobo from "I Am A Lonesome Hobo", on the other hand, is not really a homeless wanderer, but a protagonist who chooses the image of an orphaned vagabond to describe his current, desolate state of mind.

The vast majority of reviewers, both professional and unpaid enthusiasts, miss the opportunity to roam endless distances with the obvious fact that the poet here uses *lonely tramp* only in a transferable way. Woody Guthrie is brought in, reference is made to the age-old archetype in songs that the wanderer is, and in fact only one single Christian exegete tries to look behind that wanderer's mask. "The Devil," Ben Cartwright suspects (in *The Telegraph* # 49, 1994), or at least a narrator who has been seduced by Satan.

But the mere fact that this is the only unsympathetic hobo in Dylan's entire oeuvre might reveal that this protagonist is not a real wanderer, but - for example - a retired businessman looking back on his life. And then establishes how all commercial successes and all material gain have cost him true happiness; he is lonely and unloved and has no real home. The price, he now sees, was too high. An edifying song text, all in all, the message of which could have come flawlessly from Luke The Drifter - apart from the confusing, Kafkaesque, moralizing finale, of course.

III   The Zimmerman Shadow

The song is and remains, despite all its simple beauty, a neglected child. Dylan plays it five times in the studio (the fifth take is the final one) and never again. Just as lukewarm is the colleagues' love; there are not too many covers. To compensate: almost every cover is very attractive.

The oldest cover is quite obscure and is recorded a few months after the original, in 1968, by old friends Brian Auger Trinity & Julie Driscoll, known for the extremely successful, now classic Basement hit "This Wheel's Of Fire". Their very groovy "I Am A Lonesome Hobo" is actually as seductive and has an equally antiquarian charm today, but at the time neither Brian Auger nor the record company believe in it. The recording is not used for the album *Open* (thankfully, their irresistible version of Donovan's "Season Of The Witch" does withstand the selection), and is merely released as a single in France. Only in 1999 does the gem appear on the collection *The Mod Years: 1965-1969*.

At the other end of the spectrum stands the austere, folky version of Thea Gilmore, on her beautiful, respectful tribute project *John Wesley Harding* (2011), according to the native of Oxford Dylan's "most sustained and satisfying record." Only with banjo and guitar. *And* with Thea's breathless, ethereal singing, of course.

The old-fashioned approach is also preferred by Dylan veteran Duke Robillard, on his thirty-fifth (!) studio album *Ear Worms*, 2019. The slow, slightly lurid reading reveals how the song would have sounded if Dylan had written it around *Time Out Of Mind* and had recorded it with Robillard and producer Daniel Lanois in New Orleans. Fortunately, Duke does not sing himself. Co-Rhode Islander Mark Cutler helps him out.

Completely different and just as pleasant is the energetic, compelling approach of The Triffids, the new-wave band from Perth, Australia. Hidden on their forgotten 1983 debut album, *Treeless Plain*, it stands the test of time. It is also the shortest version of "I Am A Lonesome Hobo"; more than a minute shorter than the master's 3'24" and much shorter than the longest cover, the 5'33" of the lamented guitar genius Jef Lee Johnson.

Jef Lee Johnson (1958-2013) plays during his rich but too short career with jazz greats like McCoy Tyner, with jazz funk king George Duke, with soul queen Aretha Franklin and pop virtuoso Billy Joel, he plays in the house band of David Letterman and tours with R&B talent Erykah Badu. But in 2009, four years before his death, he reveals on his tribute album *The Zimmerman Shadow* where his deepest love lies: with Dylan.

The album definitely deserves a place in an imaginary Top 10 of Best Dylan Tribute Albums. The eleven Dylan covers on the record (nine actually; from "Knockin' On Heaven's Door", Jef Lee delivers three - sublime - versions) are all surprising and sparkling, inspiring wildly fanning jazz rock here ("As I Went Out One Morning"), and modest, sultry declarations of love there ("Idiot Wind", "Blind Willie McTell") proving, just like the jazz arrangements of Michael Moore's *Jewels And Binoculars*, Dylan right, in *Chronicles*: "Musicians have always known that my songs were about more than just words."

And a musician Jef Lee Johnson truly was. In the parable *and* in reality.

III   Wednesday November 29, 1967

"The songs of *John Wesley Harding* were all written down as poems, and the tunes were found later," Dylan says in the 1971 interview with Minnesota friend Dave Glover.

The Scottish *poet from the thirteenth century* is Sir Thomas de Ercildoun, the Scottish laird who is better known as *Thomas the Rhymer*. He acquired enough fame and awe with his poetic prophecies, even centuries after his death in 1298, but he is truly immortal thanks to Child Ballad 37, as the literary protagonist of the ballad "Thomas Rymer and Queen of Elfland".

In the ballad, the fairy Queen takes him away, and when Thomas returns seven years later, he has been given the gift of prophecy, as well as the inability to tell a lie. Hence his other nickname: *True Thomas*.

The very opening already suggests that the spirit of Thomas the Rhymer descended seven centuries later in Bob the Rhymer;

> As Thomas lay on Huntlie banks
> A wat a weel bred man was he
> And there he spied a lady fair,
> Coming riding down by the Eildon tree.

... which echoes in 1967 in Dylan's *"I spied the fairest damsel"*, from the third verse of "As I Went Out One Morning".

Thomas falls to his knees. Such a fair lady cannot be of this earth, *all hail, thou mighty Queen of Heaven! For thy peer on earth I never did see*. No, no, declares the supernatural beauty, that name does not belong to me; *I am but the queen of fair Elfland* – the same lady with whom the narrator in Dylan's "Soon After Midnight" (2012) thinks he has a chance (*"It's soon after midnight and I've got a date with a fairy queen"*).

She likes Thomas, asks for a kiss and when she gets that kiss, True Thomas is stuck with her: *"ye maun go wi me, and ye maun serve me seven years."* Then she puts him on the back of her milk-white steed, and off they ride on the long, long journey to her kingdom. On the way they rest, Thomas lays down his weary head on her lap and the Queen points at the three-way intersection:

> 'O see ye not yon narrow road,
> So thick beset with thorns and briers?
> That is the path of righteousness,
> Tho after it but few enquires.

'And see not ye that braid braid road,
That lies across that lily leven?
That is the path of wickedness,
Tho some call it the road to heaven.

... words that echo in "The Wicked Messenger" and in "The Ballad Of Frankie Lee And Judas Priest". *Judas pointed down the road and said, "Eternity (...). Though you might call it 'Paradise'."* But Thomas and the fairy queen will take the third path, the bonny road to fair Elfland.

On arrival Thomas will receive no boots of Spanish leather, but still *a pair of shoes or velvet green*. Not bad either.

Wednesday 29 November 1967, again three weeks later, again Nashville, again half a day of recording - the last one, this time. Dylan arrives with two songs, "The Wicked Messenger" and "Dear Landlord". But the spirit of Sir Thomas de Ercildoun has left Bob the Rhymer in the meantime. Dylan has to write the last two songs of the album on the spot, presumably at the Ramada Inn, where he is staying and where he introduced Bob Johnston to the songs for the new album six weeks ago.

For "Down Along The Cove" the bard seems to be able to capture a few last echoes from the thirteenth century. The archaic *"I spied my true love"*, and the setting, along the cove, mirrors True Thomas' *As Thomas lay on Huntlie banks*, but then the spirit has definitely evaporated. From here on, from the second verse of "Down Along The Cove", Dylan is on his own. The final song "I'll Be Your Baby Tonight", the following country album *Nashville Skyline*, the subsequent dry years, *New Morning*, *Planet Waves*... it takes seven years, until the 1974 *Blood On The Tracks* album, before Bob the Rhymer returns from Elfland, before he is able to climb back on Pegasus, the milk-white steed.

But first we must record the last songs for *John Wesley Harding* today. Which are:

1. The Wicked Messenger

2. I'll Be Your Baby Tonight

3. Down Along The Cove

4. Dear Landlord

Bob Dylan (gitaar, piano, harmonica)
Charlie McCoy (bas)
Kenny Buttrey (drums)
Pete Drake (steel guitar)

Producer Bob Johnston

9   The Wicked Messenger

I   Give it up!

It was very early in the morning, the streets clean and deserted, I was on my way to the station. As I checked my watch against the tower clock I realized it was much later than I had thought and that I had to hurry, the shock of this discovery made me feel uncertain of the way, I wasn't very well acquainted with the town as yet, fortunately there was a policeman nearby, I ran up to him and breathlessly asked him the way. He smiled and said: "You asking me the way?" "Yes," I said, "since I can't find it myself." "Give it up! Give it up!" he said, and swung around, like someone who wants to be alone with his laughter.

(Franz Kafka, *Give It Up!* 1922)

If on *John Wesley Harding* the Bible is *Das Ich*, The Ego, as Freud would say, then Kafka is *Das Es*, The Id, the engine that is driven by a complex of unconscious desires, emotions, and urges. It defines the uncanny, alienated, dreamlike atmosphere of highlights such as "All Along The Watchtower", "Drifter's Escape" and this "The Wicked Messenger", a stifling discomfort so masterfully articulated in Kafka's stories, like in the above "Gib's auf"

Dylan does not often mention Kafka and he seems to have only a superficial knowledge of his work. John Cohen, who interviews him in 1968, specifically asks about Kafka's *Parables and Paradoxes*, to which Dylan hardly responds. But during a press conference in Rome, July 2001, Dylan states, appreciatively meant: "There's nobody like Kafka who just sits down and writes something without wanting somebody to read it."

If anything, this shows some biographical knowledge. True, Kafka did not want his work to be read. During his lifetime he only reluctantly released, on the insistence of admiring friends, a fraction of his work for publication. On his deathbed in the sanatorium he begged his friend Max Brod to destroy all the writings in his study at home (Brod ignored that and deciphered, sorted and published everything - including masterpieces such as *Der Prozeß*, The Trial, and many parables such as the above *Gib's auf!*).

Incidentally, how Dylan comes to his conclusion is puzzling; writers who do not publish their work because they do not want it to be read are by definition unknown, after all.

Nevertheless, despite the presumably superficial knowledge of Kafka's work, the parallels cannot be ignored. An obvious guess would be that both Jewish writers demonstrate their comparable, superior talent in a similar way because there happens to be a congeniality, a spiritual affinity. Kindred spirits, if you will.

Just like Kafka, Dylan's grandparents belong to a Jewish minority in the Slavic part of Europe at the beginning of the twentieth century (Dylan's grandparents flee the pogroms in Odessa in 1905, Kafka then lives in Prague). The oppression, being an outsider, the stories, the parables and the use of language from the Torah... it is cultural baggage that is shared by Kafka and Dylan, and perhaps explains the receptiveness of both men to clear but impenetrable storytelling.

II   A rather reverse order

In the same interview with John Cohen (together with Happy Traum, published in the October '68 *Sing Out*) Dylan reflects on his lyrics for *John Wesley Harding*, in particular on "All Along The Watchtower" and "The Wicked Messenger".

Cohen wants to know what Dylan thinks about traditional ballads, and whether he would also consider a song like "The Wicked Messenger" a ballad. Dylan's answer seems serious, he chooses simple language and speaks in short, clear sentences and the whole is incomprehensible - Kafka could not have done it better:

> In a sense, but the ballad form isn't there. Well the scope is there actually, but in a more compressed sense. The scope opens up, just by a few little tricks. I know why it opens up, but in a ballad in the true sense, it wouldn't open up that way. It does not reach the proportions I had intended for it.

A ballad, as Dylan teaches in the same interview, is actually the antique version of a feature film; a balladeer tells long, drawn-out stories with a real plot and main characters who perform actions about which the public forms an opinion. The plot and the actions are all plainly told, the listener does not have to find his own interpretation, the listener does not have to fill in blanks - it says what it says.

This is in line with the literary theory; there the literary ballad is defined as a *narrative poem*.

In that sense, Dylan continues, the ballads on *John Wesley Harding* are not real ballads:

> These melodies on the *John Wesley Harding* album lack this traditional sense of time. As with the third verse of "The Wicked Messenger", which opens it up, and then the time schedule takes a jump and soon the song becomes wider. One realizes that when one hears it, but one might have to adapt to it. But we are not hearing anything that isn't there; anything we can imagine is really there. The same thing is true of the song "All Along The Watchtower", which opens up in a slightly different way, in a stranger way, for here we have the cycle of events working in a rather reverse order.

Kafka all over again: clear vagueness. Or mumbo jumbo, that is of course also possible. The "time schedule takes a jump" in the third verse? The narrative structure of the third verse is identical to that of the first two couplets, the storyline from couplet 1 to couplet 2 is exactly the same as that from couplet 2 to 3.

Each couplet opens with a wide shot; in the first half of the verse in question, an all-knowing narrator outlines successively the protagonist, his living conditions and the decor. Each verse tells an anecdote in lines four to six, every fifth line expresses an interaction of the protagonist with his environment and every sixth line is a Bible paraphrase:

For his tongue it could not speak, but only flatter can be inspired by multiple passages; *flattery* is damned in about twenty places in the Bible. Because of the proximity of the word *wickedness*, Dylan's King James was probably open at Psalm 5, verse 9: "their inward part is very wickedness; their throat is an open sepulchre; they flatter with their tongue."

The soles of my feet, I swear they're burning paraphrases another Bible passage in which again the wicked are tackled; Malachi 4:3 "And ye shall tread down the wicked; for they shall be ashes under the soles of your feet."

And the final line, *If you cannot bring good news, then don't bring any*, seems to be inspired by the story of the prophet Micah, the only one of four hundred prophets who predicts that King Ahab will fare badly if he goes to war against the Syrians - all other prophets predict a resounding victory (1 Kings 22). It is not entirely conclusive though; Micha does not bring news, but predicts, and moreover does so at the express request. Ahab knows in advance that Micah never predicts anything good ("I hate him because he never prophesies anything good about me, but always bad." - 1 Kings 22: 8).

By the way: respected Dylanologists such as Andy Gill and Derek Barker who bend and twist to fit in the prophet Eli (*the wicked messenger* comes *from Eli,* after all), seem to ignore that *Eli* also means "my God", that *Eli* is God's call sign (like Jesus on the cross also calls on Him: *Eli, Eli, lama sabachtani* - My God, my God, why hast thou forsaken me?).

Despite all the ambiguity and vagueness, within "The Wicked Messenger" it is more likely that *the wicked messenger* (Proverbs 13:17) comes from God, and not from the prophet Eli. When asked by whom he is sent, he only answers "with his thumb", because his tongue could only respond with "flattery". Strange, but traceable still within the Old Testament culture and the Jewish tradition, in which one is not allowed to speak the name of God.

III   In Schrafft's

Like all lyrics on *John Wesley Harding*, the form has a classic, elegant simplicity, yet it is different. Almost all songs (eight of the twelve) consist of eight-line couplets with the rhyme scheme *abcb-defe*; a classic ballad form, indeed.

But "The Wicked Messenger" has six-line couplets and a rather unique, "open" rhyme scheme: abc**d**bc. That fourth, surprisingly non-rhyming line contributes to the open character, which Dylan may refer to when he talks about "jumps" to "open" the ballad.

Unusual, but not entirely unique. Maybe Dylan copied "For Once In My Life", until then actually the only song with this rhyme scheme. That heartbreaker from 1965, according to authority Ella Fitzgerald *a beautiful tune*, only reaches the canon after Stevie Wonder scores a huge hit with the song (October '68), but in this late summer of 1967 the walking jukebox Dylan may have heard the Tony Bennet version, or the Four Tops or The Temptations, who all score a little hit with this song in '67.

There are more indications that Dylan the poet has found this distinctive rhyme at W.H. Auden.

Dylan has already written "As I Went Out One Morning" for this same album, whose form, rhyme scheme, weird meter and title all have been copied from Auden's "As I Walked Out One Evening".

A similar impression seems "In Schrafft's" to have made. Dylan borrows the structure (the on this album unusual three six-line couplets) and, in particular, the different *abcdbc* rhyme scheme for "The Wicked Messenger":

> *Having finished the Blue-plate Special*
> *And reached the coffee stage,*
> *Stirring her cup she sat,*
> *A somewhat shapeless figure*
> *of indeterminate age*
> *In an undistinguished hat.*

It takes quite some time before Dylan himself recognizes the special beauty of the song. The dissatisfaction he expresses in that interview with John Cohen ("*It does not reach the proportions I had intended for it*") is not false modesty: it takes no less than twenty years for the song to pop up on his set list, and then it is still thanks to the persuasiveness of the men of Grateful Dead that he plays it at all. Jerry Garcia is rather fond of the song, that's why - in 1975 Garcia already plays it ten times with his hobby project Legion Of Mary, for example.

The version with Dylan, July 12, 1987 in New York, is a driving, dynamic and enthusiastic performance, but Dylan dismisses the recording for Dylan & The Dead (maybe because he makes one mistake in the lyrics), plays it two times more (both times in Italy) and then puts the song back in the bottom drawer.

But in the twenty-first century he rediscovers the song again and he plays "The Wicked Messenger" more than a hundred times. In viciously rocking, sharp versions, destroying much of the deceptive domesticity of the original from 1967, but no less attractive.

Dylan is suddenly even to such an extent charmed that he selects the song for his film *Masked And Anonymous* (2003). In the original script, the full song lyrics are typed out, but eventually a charming live performance of "Diamond Joe", the namesake of the traditional he plays on *Good As I Been To You* (1992), appears on that particular spot in the film.

It is unknown why Dylan commits this intervention (like "All Along The Watchtower", "Trying To Get To Heaven" and "Standing In The Doorway" all reach the script, but not the final filming), but is likely that the filmmaker Dylan does not want interference; the ambiguity of "The Wicked Messenger" pushes the film interpretation somewhat too blatantly to messianic distances, probably. To distances he avoids with a "Diamond Joe", anyway.

IV   Wondering Which Way To Go

The song is fairly popular with colleagues and that produces enough beautiful covers. The soulful adaptation by Rod Stewart with his Faces, the opening track of their debut *First Step* (1970), is rightly praised.

Patti Smith opts for an ominous, solemn and gradually derailing approach, pushing the song in a completely different direction - which suits the song well (*Gone Again*, 1996). In terms of atmosphere comparable to the garage sound the Black Keys pour over it, on the successful *I'm Not There Soundtrack* (2007).

Dylan himself will be touched by Marion Williams' version, by one of the best gospel singers of the twentieth century. Williams' "Blowin' In The Wind" from '66 is already one of the few successful covers of this worn monument, her "I Shall Be Released" is superb, and especially her unparalleled, brilliant reading of "I Pity The Poor Immigrant" (1969) is goose bumps inducing. Her "The Wicked Messenger" comes close to that - from the magnificent 1971 album *Standing Here Wondering Which Way To Go*, an intersection of the best that gospel, soul and blues have to offer, and whose title song should be the soundtrack of the film version to Kafka's "Gib's auf!"

10 I'll Be Your Baby Tonight

I Blues In The Night

Somewhere in the last part of his *Black Coffee Blues* trilogy, in "Smile, You're Traveling" (2000), the multifaceted phenomenon Henry Rollins expresses his love for Sinatra, and specifically for his 50s albums:

> I like the records he did where he's all bummed out like In the Wee Small Hours, No One Cares, Where Are You and Only the Lonely. I like Sinatra because all his life he's been saying fuck all you motherfuckers with the talent to back it up. He kept coming back no matter what was thrown his way. He inspires me big time. He's like a swan, graceful but mean when confronted.

Fifteen years later, Elvis Costello writes a very similar declaration of love in his autobiography, in *Unfaithful Music & Disappearing Ink*:

> I spent nights deep in The Wee Small Hours of the Morning, No One Cares, and Only the Lonely, that incredible run of intense ballad albums that Sinatra had cut for Capitol with Nelson Riddle.

Dylan confesses that same love a little more indirectly, in *Chronicles*, when he goes all the way to describe his awe for the song "Ebb Tide": "The lyrics were so mystifying and stupendous. When Frank sang that song, I could hear everything in his voice — death, God and the universe, everything."

"Ebb Tide" is on Side 2 of *Frank Sinatra Sings For Only The Lonely* (1958) and traces of that album can be found throughout Dylan's entire oeuvre. In songs like "Forgetful Heart", "Dignity" and "Wallflower" resonate word choice and song structure, *Only The Lonely* songs like "One For My Baby (And One More For The Road)" and "Good-Bye" are paraphrased in the Basement, in "Sign Language", in "Scarlet Town" and in "Don't Think Twice", and with some cut and paste work, the classic "Blues In The Night" can be reconstructed in its entirety from Dylan's Collected Works.

"Blues In The Night" should be somewhere on the first pages of *The Great American Songbook*. Even composer Harold Arlen, usually a modest man who can't be caught on self-congratulatory behaviour, gets excited again when his biographer Edward Jablonski asks about this song: "I knew in my guts that this was strong, strong, strong!" (*Rhythm, Rainbow And Blues*, 1996). He even takes, very unusual, credit for some of the lyrics by Johnny Mercer:

> It sounded marvelous once I got to the second stanza but that first twelve was weak tea. On the third or fourth page of his work sheets I saw some lines—one of them was "My momma done tol' me, when I was in knee pants." I said, "Why don't you try that?" It was one of the very few times I've ever suggested anything like that to John.

(in Alec Wilder's American Popular Song, 1972)

True; it *is* an exceptional song. Written for the film *Hot Nocturne* in 1941, but after the success of the song the film title is changed to *Blues In The Night*. A year later, the song does not win the Academy Award for Best Song. One of the many injustices in the history of the Oscar awards, but it does get a coda.

Winner Jerome Kern ("The Last Time I Saw Paris"), who is in fact known as a quite competitive, somewhat arrogant song composer with a strong ego, is ashamed. To make up, he gives Arlen a remarkable, personal gift (the walking stick of Jacques Offenbach) and he ensures that the rules of the game are changed: from 1943, an Oscar-nominated song must actually have been written for the film. Kern's winning "The Last Time I Saw Paris" was an old song that, more or less coincidentally, was inserted at the last minute in the film *Lady Be Good*. Not an Oscar winner, as Kern himself thought at the time, so he wasn't even present at the award ceremony.

Dylan is a fan of lyricist Johnny Mercer, and especially of this song, although in *Chronicles* he still seems to think it's all Harold Arlen:

> Arlen had written "The Man That Got Away" and the cosmic "Somewhere Over the Rainbow", another song by Judy Garland. He had written a lot of other popular songs, too — the powerful "Blues in the Night", "Stormy Weather", "Come Rain or Come Shine", "Get Happy". In Harold's songs, I could hear rural blues and folk music. There was an emotional kinship there.

Of course, Guthrie, Hank Williams, Hank Snow... they are all deeper under his skin, "but I could never escape from the bittersweet, lonely, intense world of Harold Arlen."

Copywriter Johnny Mercer does not get explicit credits from the bard, but indirectly more than once. From this song, from "Blues In The Night", the Dylan fan recognizes

> *Now the rain's a-fallin'*
> *Hear the train a-callin'*

... of which echoes descend in "A Hard Rain's A-Gonna Fall" and in "Dusty Old Fairgrounds". The fourth verse opens with

> *From Natchez to Mobile*
> *From Memphis to St. Joe*

... that should sound familiar too, and the chorus,

> *The evenin' breeze'll start the trees to cryin'*
> *And the moon'll hide it's light*
> *When you get the blues in the night*
> *Take my word, the mockingbird'll sing the saddest kind of song*
> *He knows things are wrong, and he's right*

... reveals where Dylan borrowed that atypical combination of *moon* and *mockingbird* from "I'll Be Your Baby Tonight" (and that last line comes very close to "You're Gonna Make Me Lonesome", first verse - *when something's not right, it's wrong*).

II   Slut wives

Together with "Down Along The Cove", "I'll Be Your Baby Tonight" is the odd song out on *John Wesley Harding*. After ten songs with mysterious, biblical, parable-like lyrics such as "All Along The Watchtower", "Drifter's Escape" and "Dear Landlord", the album closes with two genuine country songs, both love songs with simple language, simple lyrics without extravagancies like *barefoot servants*, *fairest damsels* or obscure saints wrapped in *solid gold*, and they are the only songs on the record in which a steel guitar plays along (Pete Drake).

In retrospects and review articles, the songs are often referred to as "transition songs", as a transition to, or some sort of strategic, announcement of the country on the next album, on *Nashville Skyline*. Dylan himself does not agree with that, not with the assumption that he would have a preconceived strategy, that at the time of *John Wesley Harding* he would already have had ideas about the next album. But, obviously, it is undeniable that both songs would fit on *Nashville Skyline* without any problems.

The last two songs are also recorded last, written last and, unlike the other ten songs, written on the spot, where according to Dylan music and lyrics came simultaneously - for the other songs he had written the lyrics well before.

Thus, the Spirit of Nashville, the world's country capital, finally gets hold of Dylan after all. Ironic, because Dylan himself had just relieved the city of that stamp by recording *Blonde On Blonde* in Nashville. The previously prevailing provincialism and the one-sidedness of the music scene before *Blonde On Blonde* the reminiscing autobiographer expresses, rather crassly, in *Chronicles*:

> The town was like being in a soap bubble. They nearly ran
> Al Kooper, Robbie Robertson and me out of town for
> having long hair. All the songs coming out of the studios
> then were about slut wives cheating on their husbands or
> vice versa.

... and "I'll Be Your Baby Tonight" is not that far behind. Admittedly, the text is vague enough to be able to deny adultery is committed here. With some creativity one could even say that the sung *Baby* is literally a baby, that Dylan is writing a lullaby for the one and a half year old Jesse Dylan. But Ockham's razor points to the most obvious interpretation: an I-person who sings *"I'll be your sweetheart tonight"* is not the lawful life partner of the sung - but probably a *slut wife cheating on her husband or vice versa*.

III   All that jazz

Totally unimportant, of course. "I'll Be Your Baby Tonight" is a beautiful song, with the shine of an indestructible evergreen, which is almost immediately recognized by the front fighters of both the country and pop world.

The superpower Burl Ives records his version as early as 1968, a few months after the release of *John Wesley Harding*, for his album *The Times They Are A-Changin'*, on which he covers no fewer than four Dylan songs (also "One Too Many Mornings" and "Don't Think Twice It's All Right" - Burl writes it without a comma).

The covers are rather controversial. Producer is Dylan expert Bob Johnston, who recorded the original a few months before. The album is recorded in the same studio in Nashville and though the sleeve does not mention musicians, it is likely that the Nashville Cats Charlie McCoy and Kenny Buttrey are on duty again. But it is arranged quite horribly, with tormenting violins, corny female choirs and a theatrically talk-singing Ives.

"I'll Be Your Baby Tonight" is the exception. It's not too bad - Burl sings without the talk, the violins hold back - it is rightly chosen as a single and it is both in America and in Australia a modest hit (numbers 35 and 28 respectively).

Equally eager are Emmylou Harris, Ray Stevens, George Baker, Anne Murray and many more artists; before 1970, within two years, half the premier division already has the song on the repertoire.

The popularity does not decrease after 1970. "I'll Be Your Baby Tonight" is undoubtedly high on a (non-existent) list of Most Covered Dylan Songs, and is often chosen as a single. The Hollies, Judy Rodman, Bobby Darin, John Walker (of the Walker Bothers), Blossom Toes ... that list is endless too.

The biggest success is the one-off project Robert Palmer & UB40, which achieves a major hit in 1990 with a tolerable, cute reggae arrangement of the song.

Dylan's heart probably skipped a beat when Hank Williams Jr., the son of his great hero, covered the song. Only for sentimental reasons, however - Hank's cover is intolerably smooth.

Unreal, and much more fun, is the former Deep Purple singer Ian Gillan, turning it into a cheerful, cajun-like sing-along (on *Gillan's Inn*, 2006).

But real beauty, real moving power cannot be found that often. For the time being this is limited to two almost perfect masterpieces, both of which also manage to extract something from the original that Dylan himself only partly achieves.

The first, and actually the best, is Norah Jones, the exceptionally talented daughter of Ravi Shankar, who also sings such a crushing "Heart Of Mine". Her "I'll Be Your Baby Tonight" is sultry, a bit ordinary and sexy - exactly what the song calls for. On *Stay With Me*, 2003.

Well alright, of equal merit is the rendition of Curtis Stigers, not coincidentally also from the jazz corner, with a cool swinging, lazy jazz performance - even better live than the studio version (*Real Emotion*, 2007).

Apparently Dylan, despite the unmistakable country overtones, injected subcutaneously *Wee Small Hours*. A *Blues In The Night* is hidden in it, which only the real jazz talents are able to uncover.

11   Down Along The Cove

I   Bob Johnston

Producer Bob Johnston's work ethic is absurd as it is, but the production he runs in 1969 exceeds the absurd. Dylan's *Nashville Skyline*, Leonard Cohen's *Songs From A Room*, The Byrds (*Dr. Byrds & Mr. Hyde*), Dan Hicks, two Johnny Cash records (*The Holy Land* and *At San Quentin*), Marty Robbins, Flat & Scruggs, Moby Grape ... and this is still an incomplete list.

He brings it on himself. He deliberately plans recording sessions for Dylan and Cash on the same day, hoping that the two giants will meet each other and perhaps then, in a cheerful mood, record some songs together. It does mean that Johnston works twenty-hour days, but it pays off (officially we won't hear the result until 2019, on *The Bootleg Series Vol. 15: Travelin 'Thru, 1967–1969*).

And when Moby Grape calls, the band is told that he has exactly three days (27, 28 and 29 May) to record an entire album with them - take it or leave it and find another producer (the result, *Truly Fine Citizen*, is clearly a rush job, but still truly fine).

Busy, busy. Yet, when Ches Millican of Epic Records in London calls Johnston in March '69 to ask if he can do the new single for Georgie Fame, Johnston says: "Sure." He gets on the plane and even makes time in London for an interview with *Melody Maker* (March 15, 1969):

> I told CBS I'd give him a Top 10 record, and then give him one in the States. They said would I like to put that on paper, and I said I would. I've got a couple of Dylan's songs for him and we'll make the final choice from three I have in mind.

Johnston is still employed by CBS in those days, which may explain this atypical big talk about that guaranteed "Top 10 hit". He probably feels like a few days of working holiday on the other side of the ocean, and this is how he sells the "working holiday" to his boss.

In the Wessex Studios at Highbury New Park (within hearing distance of Arsenal, so no recordings are made during matches) a super trio is ready for the basic tracks: apart from Georgie Fame also Jack Bruce's armoured concrete bass from, who now has some spare time in between the breakup of Cream (November '68) and his first solo album (*Songs For A Tailor*, September 1969), and England's best session guitarist, legendary Chris Spedding (who will also assist Jack Bruce on his solo albums).

Johnston records two Dylansongs with the men. The third song, the song he says he "has in mind", is unknown, but a year later Chris Spedding records his own solo album *Backwood Progression*, with a surprising version of the then rather obscure Basement song "Please Mrs. Henry ".

Recorded will be the B-side of the upcoming single, "I'll Be Your Baby Tonight". That is, after the original with Bob Dylan and the somewhat dubious cover by Burl Ives for his peculiar LP *The Times They Are A-Changin'* (1968), already Johnston's third professional studio recording of the same song within a year and a half. Georgie Fame gives it a completely misplaced, but still infectious, very Londonesque Swinging Sixties twist.

And the A-side of the "guaranteed Top-10 hit" will be that other maverick from *John Wesley Harding*: "Down Along The Cove".

II   The Jacks and the River Queen

It is a brave choice. Of the two odd ducks out, "Down Along The Cove" is the ugly duckling. The hit potential and charm of "I'll Be Your Baby Tonight" are recognized from day one and since then confirmed almost continuously, but "Down Along The Cove" is not only skipped by almost the entire music world, but is also ignored by the master himself - it takes no less than twenty-two years, until 1999, before he finally performs the song.

Successfully and satisfactorily, by the way: until 2006 it is on the set list more than seventy times.

With a remarkable twist, though. Already at the premiere, in 1999, almost all words are different. In 2003 Dylan introduces a completely revised, twice as long text. Lyrics changes as such are not that special, but the poet's official stamp is quite exceptional; apparently, he finds the text revision so important that he has the new text included in the next edition of *Lyrics*, in *Lyrics 1962-2001* (2004). Only one other example of such a manoeuvre is known - "Gonna Change My Way Of Thinking", the *Slow Train Coming* song from 1979. Of both songs, the revised second versions are since 2004 officially printed after the original lyrics as "alternate versions" and also published on the site. The copyright of the rewritten "Down Along The Cove" was established in 2002.

Mysterious. The lyrics of a cathedral like "Tangled Up In Blue" change continuously and much more drastically, Dylan himself declares the *Real Live* version (1984) "more like it should have been, the imagery is better" but even that doesn't move him to officially changing the lyrics accordingly. The revised text is more than twice as long (from three to six verses, but also from 106 to 230 words), and only the "Down along the cove I spied my little bundle of joy" line is maintained.

The original lyrics are not very inspired and not surprising, that is true. In the first verse he sees his true love walking along the water, in the second verse this bundle of joy, his sweet son apparently, and in the third verse the beloved and he walk, in love and all, hand in hand "down along the cove", along that creek. No outlaws, no saints, jokers, thieves or vagrants, no mysterious, loaded dialogues or ominous set pieces ... not only musically "Down Along The Cove" marks a radical break with the previous ten songs on *John Wesley Harding*, but lyrically too, all in all.

This may be an explanation for Dylan's remarkable intervention; refine it a little to make it fit a little better. That "bit of refinement" then gets a bit out of hand (it is a complete renovation plus annexe) and anyway: renovation would be a pointless motivation (the album is the album, after all), but the spirit of the lyrics changes seems to indicate so.

The second verse introduces "a bunch of people" with evil intentions - similar to the nameless, intimidating groups of people in "Drifter's Escape", "I Am A Lonesome Hobo" and "The Wicked Messenger".

The exclamation "Lord have mercy" is promoted to recurring refrain line and is now at the end of each verse (like *he was never known* in the song "John Wesley Harding").

Couplets are now enriched with enigmatic, moralistic rhetoric such as

> *They're gonna knock you when you're up*
> *They're gonna kick you when you're down*

... and above all: the poet Dylan pushes the whole song back a century, to the nineteenth century, to the time of the Wild West.

He does so by using a decor piece that we still know from his old song "Rambling, Gambling Willie" from 1962:

> *Sailin' down the Mississippi to a town called New Orleans,*
> *They're still talkin' about their card game on that Jackson River Queen.*
> *"I've come to win some money," Gamblin' Willie says,*
> *When the game finally ended up, the whole damn boat was his.*
> *And it's ride, Willie, ride,*
> *Roll, Willie, roll,*
> *Wherever you are a-gamblin' now, nobody really knows.*

... so, the *Jackson River Queen* casino boat, the famous steamboat that sails up and down the Misssissippi and is apparently gambled away by the captain to that darn Willie. The boat never existed, by the way. Dylan ties together the names of two famous nineteenth-century river boats (the *River Queen* and the *General Jackson*).

His intention to insert that mood-determining boat almost fails, partly due to his own negligence. Incomprehensibly Dylan leaves the transcription of the new text to the same hard-of-hearing dyslexic who also hears *"Cold black water dog"* in "Tell me, Momma" and *"because the bird is here and you might want to enter it"* in "Sign On The Cross" (and dozens of other horrors).

Here the transcriptor on duty makes a slightly less colourful mess: *The Jacks and the River Queen*. But it remains odd that Dylan, who apparently makes it a point that this revised text is included in the new edition of the official *Lyrics*, allows such a hare-brained transcription to pass again. And again. The corruption has still not been corrected in the next edition of *Lyrics* (2016) nor on the site. On the stage he sings in any case:

> *Down along the cove I seen the Jackson River Queen*
> *Down along the cove I seen the Jackson River Queen*
> *I said, "Lord have mercy, baby*
> *Ain't that the biggest boat you ever seen?"*

The boat has no further substantive function, so is apparently only used as a set piece, is only mentioned to move the entire song back to the second half of the nineteenth century, to the time of *John Wesley Harding*.

The other, less drastic style break in "Down Along The Cove" is rightly praised: the use of steel guitarist Pete Drake. The music of the ten songs before this one is provided by the trio Dylan (guitar and harmonica), drummer Kenny Buttrey and Charlie McCoy on bass.

For this song Dylan takes place at the piano (for the second time, after "Dear Landlord" and for the first time a fourth musician, Pete Drake, is admitted. In the first verse, Drake limits himself to short, beat-like, percussive accents, causing the listener to hear a normal electric guitar in the first instance, but then he draws his long, dramatic lines and short, melodic licks over the strings - pushing the record for the first time towards more traditional country. Kenny Buttrey wakes up, racing over the toms as in his best "Absolutely Sweet Marie" moments.

III   Duane & Duke

Ignored, but not completely ignored, this "Down Along The Cove".

Guitar legend Davey Graham (back then still "Davy") uses the song as a framework for his virtuosity on the album *Hat* (1969), and as an unlikely bridge between his guitar arrangement of Purcell's baroque "Hornpipe for Harpsichord" and Willie Dixon's blues classic "Hoochie Coochie Man".

Closer to the source is Duane Allman's approach in 1970, on the album *Ton-Ton Macoute!*. Originally intended as a solo album but turned into a Johnny Jenkins record - solid Southern Blues Rock, as can be expected from the Allman just before the founding of the Allman Brothers. An elegant echo of that exercise sounds forty-one years later, forty years after Duane's death, as Steely Dan frontman and loyal Dylan fan Donald Fagen surprisingly enters the stage at a concert of the Allman Brothers Band in New York (March 17, 2011). He sings and plays "Down Along The Cove", Duane's brilliant play on the slide guitar is masterfully provided by his true heir, Derek Trucks.

A little earlier in the twenty-first century, in 2006, one of Dylan's session musicians records the best cover: the tireless, ever-running guitarist Duke Robillard, on his *Groove-A-Rama* album - an irresistible, smoothly swinging rockabilly arrangement of "Down Along The Cove".

The smooth swing also has the legendary Bob Johnston production of Georgie Fame's cover, plus the very Londonesque Swinging Sixties charm of heavy horns and groovy background singers.

It won't be a Top 10 hit though. Neither Top 20. Georgie Fame's "Down Along The Cove" never even scratched the hit parade at all.

But he did make an impression still. When a few months later, August 1969, Dylan is in England for the performance at Wight, a reporter asks if he would like to meet anyone here in England.

> "I'm hoping to meet anybody who's around. I'd like to meet The Who and maybe Georgie Fame."

12   Dear Landlord

I   Neil Young

When John Kiernan returns home from shopping, he sees two strangers standing in front of his house. He is not particularly alarmed. "Neil Young fan alert," he says to his wife Patti Regan. Kiernan and Patti live in Winnipeg, as it so happens to be in the house where Neil Young grew up, and they are used to fans watching their home. While Patti puts the groceries in, John goes to chat with both men. They were a bit older than your typical Young fan, Kiernan remembers later. And while chatting, he notices that guy with the big cap is wearing really beautiful cowboy boots and cool leather pants. He studies his face closer and "it suddenly occurred to me that I was talking to Bob Dylan."

The landlord asks if Bob wants to see inside the house, and Dylan is eager. Patti takes the men upstairs, to the former teenage room of Neil, now a pink painted girl's room of their sixteen-year-old daughter.

"So, this is the room where he was listening to his music," Dylan muses, "and this was his view."

The bard hangs around for some twenty minutes, they talk about Neil Young, about the places in Winnipeg where he probably performed with his school band, the weather and life in the North. Then Dylan and his companion get back in the taxi that has been waiting in front of the house all this time, and leave.

> "You were pretty cool talking to a huge celebrity," John compliments his wife.
> "What celebrity?" Patti asks.
> "Bob Dylan."
> "That's why he looked so familiar to me!" Patti screams and runs wildly waving and yelling to the neighbours who are raking leaves in the front yard. "There in that cab! Bob Dylan is in the cab!"

This takes place November 2, 2008, and John Kiernan cherishes the memory of the day he could do Bob Dylan a favour.

The in itself futile event touches a chord. The *Winnipeg Free Press* writes an article on it and in the course of the next weeks, media around the world deem it worthy a report. Understandable, actually; it is moving somehow, the world's greatest songwriter, who, like an adoring fan is contemplating his idol in some girl's bedroom.

Dylan's respect and friendly feelings for Neil Young are well known. The sympathetic name-check in "Highlands" (1997, 'I'm listening to Neil Young / I gotta turn up the sound') does not come out of the blue - since the early seventies Dylan says nice, admiring things about the Canadian, occasionally joins him on stage and in his autobiography (*Waging Heavy Peace: A Hippie Dream*, 2012) Young confirms that Dylan sometimes comes over for dinner, that they call every now and then and that Dylan occasionally sends over gifts.

One time, however, in 1985, Dylan's grapes are sour:

> The only time it bothered me that someone sounded like me was when I was living in Phoenix, Arizona, in about '72 and the big song at the time was Heart Of Gold. I used to hate it when it came on the radio. I always liked Neil Young, but it bothered me every time I listened to Heart Of Gold. I think it was up at number one for a long time, and I'd say, 'Shit, that's me. If it sounds like me, it should as well be me.' There I was, stuck on the desert someplace, having to cool out for a while. New York was a heavy place. Woodstock was worse, people living in trees outside my house, fans trying to batter down my door, cars following me up dark mountain roads. I needed to lay back for a while, forget about things, myself included, and I'd get so far away and turn on the radio and there I am, but it's not me. It seemed to me somebody else had taken my thing and had run away with it, you know, and I never got over it.

This is during Dylan's dry period, in the years that he hardly makes music. In this particular period he might be more petty, more sensitive in this area, but he does have a point:

that thin harmonica, Kenny Buttrey on drums, Nashville, the austere production ... yes, it could have been a *John Wesley Harding* song. Somewhere between "Dear Landlord", the song in which Dylan sounds like Neil Young, and the last two songs, "Down Along The Cove" and "I'll Be Your Baby Tonight", which are so alienating, abruptly leaping to pure country, being the only songs accompanied by a steel guitar, like "Heart Of Gold".

II   Triptych

"Dear Landlord" is a pearl that shines even more outside the context of *John Wesley Harding*. On the album itself, between all those beautiful songs with similar structure, instrumentation and atmosphere, the song tends to drown a bit. Dylan selects it in 1985 for *Biograph* and here, between "Mr. Tambourine Man" and "It Ain't Me, Babe" the song comes more into its own.

Dylan's own comment in the accompanying booklet is just as skimpy as the arrangement: "Dear Landlord was really just the first line. I woke up one morning with the words on my mind. Then I just figured, what else can I put to it?"

It *is* a beautiful, dark and foreboding first line. 'Dear landlord' is enough to evoke a naturalistic drama, or a bitter Woody Guthrie ballad, proletarians misery and crisis years atmosphere. And the word *landlord* has a double entendre to it, opens even more vistas - the road is paved towards religious associations or ironic portraits. Subsequently, most of the interpreters are moving exactly in that direction.

The pathetic A.J. Weberman, the stalking fool who even goes through Dylan's garbage, thinks he can prove that the lyrics are settling accounts with manager Albert Grossman, who actually, literally, is Dylan's landlord (from Dylan's house in Woodstock). Interpretations of the years after Dylan's Christian phase, that is after 1981, are mainly leaning towards a religious interpretation. Well, at least there are more tangible handles supporting those perceptions: just like in nine songs surrounding this one, in "Dear Landlord" Bible quotations do echo. In majority from the New Testament, by the way, but not only from the four Gospels; Dylan keeps on browsing, through Romans and Corinthians in particular. 1Cor. 7:7, for example: 'every man hath his proper gift'.

Conclusive none of them are, those dozens of readings. That is not surprising either, if one is to trust Dylan's own words, taking into account verse 4: *my dreams are beyond control*. The poet has, after the night has given him the two words *dear landlord*, unlocked the gates to his subconscious and lets the stream of consciousness flow. It yields these three fascinating couplets, full of Kafkaesque guiltless guilt, clear and lucid, but impenetrable. In addition, Bible fragments, a phrase from an old song by Roy Acuff (*when that steamboat whistle blows* almost literally derives from "Steamboat Whistle Blues", 1936) and archaic, Biblical clichés like *my burden is heavy* and *heed these words*.

The overall picture is a triptych, depicting three times a pitiful debtor who begs a higher authority to spare him. What that debt consists of and who the landlord is remains open, just like in Kafka's stories. But granted, a thoroughly Christian setting, a triptych such as *The Last Judgment* by Lucas van Leyden (1527) fits well.

III   Old Man

In 1969, Janis Joplin turns the song into a steamy, soulful blues rock exercise and completely misfires, of course - but it still has the surreptitious attraction of a guilty pleasure. That is less true for the comparable, but slightly safer Joe Cocker (also '69). The song hangs in the air that year; Fairport Convention also picks it up for the masterpiece *Unhalfbricking*, but ultimately does not select it. Defensible - Sandy Denny sings great, but the accompaniment of Richard Thompson and his men is a bit lukewarm.

In the twenty-first century the Joan Baez rip-off from Wales Debbie Clarke attracts attention. Far too sterile, but the fact that she dares to choose "Dear Landlord" speaks for her, of course (*Manhattanhenge*, 2012, produced by the man-behind-Bowie Tony Visconti).

Closer to the source, because much rawer and frayed, is Mirah and the Black Cat Orchestra from Seattle (*To All We Stretch The Open Arm*, 2004). For the time being, however, Thea Gilmore's version, on her dazzling tribute album *John Wesley Harding* (2002), with beautiful dobro guitar, continues to lead the women's and men's competition.

For the time being, because Neil Young has yet to do his thing. Dylan is now over it, over that "Heart Of Gold". Has even played Young's "Old Man" on the stage a few times. The way is clear. The steamboat whistle blows.

IV   Frank is the key

Question: What is your message?
Dylan: Keep a good head and always carry a light bulb.
(26 April 1965, Press Conference, London, England)

For a short while, it is a running gag, in the spring of '65. Dylan arrives at Heathrow and is speaking to the press in a waiting room. The attention is drawn by an oversized industrial lightbulb in Dylan's hand. When asked, Dylan declares that he received the lightbulb from *a very affectionate friend* and a moment later it inspires him to the above message to the English people. And more than two weeks later he still finds it an inspiring image, apparently. To interviewer Alan Coleman, still in London, he reveals:

> Everybody has their own idea of what's a poet. Robert Frost, President Johnson, T.S. Eliot, Rudolph Valentino – they're all poets. I like to think of myself as the one who carried the lightbulb.

A final echo the joke has in the liner notes of *John Wesley Harding*.

For the back-cover Dylan has written a parable-like story, of which the opening promises an abundance of interpretation possibilities:

> There were three kings and a jolly three too. The first one had a broken nose, the second, a broken arm and the third was broke. "Faith is the key!" said the first king. "No, froth is the key!" said the second. "You're both wrong," said the third, "the key is Frank!"

A real windfall for eager Dylan exegetes with cryptanalytic ambitions. "Three Kings" has a biblical connotation, the enumeration of their handicaps a metaphorical quality, the successive assignments of "faith", "froth" and "Frank" as being "the key" predicts an allegorical turn and the whole thing is stylistically a fairy tale... and we are only 52 words underway.

Anyway, Frank. When we get there, we first witness a symbolic content insinuating dialogue between Frank's housemates "Vera" and "Terry Shute". The script assigns Terry mainly biblically charged text. Terry is not a fan of the three kings. He thinks the trio is a "motley crew", and he speaks badly of them in their presence, in Matthew paraphrases: "They ask nothing and they receive nothing" (Matt. 7:8), "Forgiveness is not in them" (Matt. 6:15), and with slang borrowed from Matthew such as "they shall not prevail", "scorn" and "wilderness". Frank, a bit fed up with Terry's whining, gets rid of him, in some sort of biblical style: "Come ye no more".

Now the kings can tell what they want from Frank. *The key* the kings need, is the key to *Mr. Dylan's new record*. With some tolerance, we see for the first time some coherence in the parable. So far, the story is Kafkaesque, no sentence follows the previous one logically in terms of content, but now we can at least place those handicaps from the opening;

> - the first king has a broken nose, so he lacks a sense to understand Mr. Dylan's record;
> - the second king has a broken arm and is therefore unable to grasp the album;
> - the third king is broke, so lacks the means to understand *John Wesley Harding*.

It would have been easy enough for Frank to deny that he is the key. After all, already in the opening song, the title song "John Wesley Harding", the bard reveals that the outlaw is the key: "*He opened many a door*". But Frank plays along, and confirms when asked that he is, indeed, the key.

In that case, ask the kings, can you let us in just a little bit? "Just far enough so's we can say we've been there." Magnanimously, Frank is not unwilling to comply with this request. But alas, the key is not very enlightening - at least not for the reader:

> First of all, he sat down and crossed his legs, then he sprung up, ripped off his shirt and began waving it in the air. A lightbulb fell from one of his pockets and he stamped it out with his foot. Then he took a deep breath, moaned and punched his fist through the plate-glass window. Settling back in his chair, he pulled out a knife, "Far enough?" he asked.

Yes, apparently it is far enough; for when the kings have left the building, the nose is fixed, the arm is healed, and king 3 is rich again.

Frank's "key" is in line with Dylan's lyrics in these years, with the course of interactions in songs such as "Ballad Of A Thin Man", "Fourth Time Around" and "Please Mrs. Henry", for example. Just as Mr. Jones from "Ballad Of A Thin Man" is confronted with grotesque answers to his normal questions, Frank "answers" grotesquely to the question of the kings.

And it is in line with the absurdities with which Dylan tackles journalists' questions. (Q: *What's the reason for your visit to California?* Dylan: Oh, I'm here looking for some donkeys. I am making a movie about Jesus).

At the same time, however, Frank's answer is a closing line underneath the absurdities and the grotesque. This is the last time a lightbulb turns up, the attribute that the mercury Dylan two years ago claimed you should always carry with you. Apparently, Frank does, but then, when the bulb falls out of his pocket, it is destroyed, deliberately and permanently. The symbolism-seeking Dylan interpreter jumps up: Aha! A farewell to an era! The Age Of The Lightbulb is over.

Just as obvious and clichéd is Frank's next dramatic action, the smashing of the glass window. The window is gone now. No longer can we "look inside". "I put myself out of the songs. I'm not in the songs anymore," as Dylan will say to John Cohen and Happy Traum a few months later, in the interview for *Sing Out!* In other words, we can no longer look inside Dylan.

And with the names, the creatives can do enough. Of course "Frank" is *sincere*, and "Vera" means *truth*, and the most persevering key seekers know how to make something out of "Terry Shute". Perhaps the most beautiful, and in any case the most creative, is the always far-fetching, admirable professor Louis Renza:

> Some critics have taken "Shute" as a thinly disguised, autobiographical reference to Bob Dylan's business manager at the time, Albert Grossman, with whom he was at odds over financial control of his work. But in allegorical terms, Terry Shute's name connotes an ironic pun on Terre Haute (Indiana) meaning "high land" or "high ground." Compared with "haute" or higher standards for his work, this "Shute" figure regards it from a decidedly second-rate, far lower perspective.

Yeah. And *Terry Shute* rhymes with *parachute*, by all means, let us not forget that.

But then again – a parable is almost by definition ambiguous, so one single correct interpretation does not exist. The Dylanologists all agree with Professor Renza on one thing though: *John Wesley Harding* is a brilliant, lonely, timeless masterpiece.

.

Sources

Well, I investigated all the books in the library
Ninety percent of 'em gotta be burned away

Dylan:

- *Writings & Drawings* (1973)

- *John Wesley Harding*

- www.bobdylan.com

- *Chronicles* (2004)

- *Masked And Anonymous (2003)*

- *Theme Time Radio Hour* (2006-08)

- *MusiCares-speech,* 2015

- *Nobel prize-speech,* 2016

Interviewfragments:

- *Every Mind Polluting Word* (collected interviews, 2006)

- *The "lost interviews and unseen letters",* Tony Glover

On Dylan (in addition to the mentioned books and sites):

- *Million Dollar Bash,* Sid Griffin, 2007, revised 2014

- *Revolution in the Air* - Clinton Heylin, 2009

- *Dylan's Autobiography of a Vocation* - Louis A. Renza, 2017 -

- *Still On The Road* - Clinton Heylin, 2010

- *Down The Highway* - Howard Sounes, 2001

- *No Direction Home* - Robert Shelton, 1986

- *Liner notes Biograph* - Cameron Crowe, 1985

- *Dylan & De Beats* – Tom Willems, 2018

- bjorner.com

- bobdylaninnederland.blogspot.nl

- expectingrain.com

Miscellaneous (in addition to the mentioned books):

- *The Life of John Wesley Hardin,* autobiography, 1896
- *Johnny Cash Sings The Ballads Of The True West*, 1965
- *Backstage Passes And Backstabbing Bastards*, Al Kooper, 1998
- *And A Voice To Sing With*, Joan Baez, 1987
- *The Collected Poetry of W.H. Auden*, 1949
- *The Strange Case of Dr Jekyll and Mr Hyde*, R.L. Stevenson, 1886
- *Testimony,* Robbie Robertson, 2016
- *This Wheel's On Fire,* Levon Helm, 1993
- *Sämtliche Erzählungen,* Kafka, 1979
- *The English and Scottish Popular Ballads*, Francis Child, 1965
- happytraum.com
- *Black Coffee Blues,* Henry Rollins, 2000
- *Unfaithful Music & Disappearing Ink*, Elvis Costello, 2015
- *Fifteen One-Act Plays,* Sam Shepard, 2012
- *The Bible -* mainly King James Version

The author

Bob Dylan's songs continue to fascinate.

Jochen Markhorst (1964) grew up in Arnhem, The Netherlands and in Hanover, Germany, and lives in Utrecht. He is not one of the hardliners who honour the motto *Nobody Sings Dylan Like Dylan* – Jimi Hendrix is certainly not the only one who can brush up a Dylan song. He preaches this controversial opinion, among other things, in his contributions to the popular English blog *Untold Dylan* and in his eleven books on Dylan songs Markhorst continues to build on the Dylan library.

Thanks

Tom Willems, from *bobdylaninnederland.blogspot.nl* - the mercury Dylan blog, the author of *Dylan & De Beats,*

Martin Bierens - dear old Bobhead in Ireland, from Utrecht to Amsterdam in Holland to Dornbirn in Austria to Stadskanaal to Tilburg to Bielefeld in Germany

Tony Attwood - webmaster of *Untold Dylan,* the place where it's always safe and warm

Larry Fyffe, appreciated ant-fucker in New Brunswick, for correcting the connecting chapters

In the same series:

  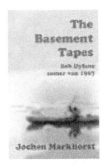

Printed in Great Britain
by Amazon

79282069R00081